Digging Deeper

*Integrating Youth Gardens
Into Schools & Communities*

A Comprehensive Guide

**Every flower of every tomorrow
is in the seeds of today.**

– CHINESE PROVERB

Digging Deeper

Integrating Youth Gardens Into Schools & Communities

A Comprehensive Guide

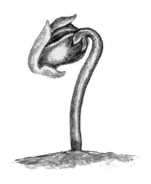

BY JOSEPH KIEFER & MARTIN KEMPLE

Foreword by Alice Waters, Author/Chef, Chez Panisse Restaurant

A Production of Food Works and the Common Roots Press
in partnership with the
American Community Gardening Association

Co-sponsored by the National Gardening Association and Let's Get Growing

Digging Deeper is a production of Food Works, the Vermont-based non-profit educational organization which offers courses, workshops, and guidebooks for creating community-based curriculum that focuses on the local natural and cultural heritage. (See page 142.)

This publication is presented in partnership with the American Community Gardening Association, a non-profit, membership organization of professionals, volunteers, and other supporters of community gardening and greening in urban, suburban, and rural areas. For more information on ACGA, write:

American Community Gardening Association
100 North 20th Street, 5th Floor
Philadelphia, PA 19103-1495
76573.262@compuserve.com

All of us at Food Works wish to express our deep gratitude to our growing family of sustained funders who have made this work possible:

The Joukowsky Family Foundation,
with a special thanks to Tim Joukowsky
and his family Peg, Lydia, and Alexandra

The L.Z. Francis Foundation

The Edwards Foundation

The Bay-Paul Foundation

The Lance Family Fund

The Freeman Foundation

The Turrell Fund

The Food-for-All Foundation

The Ben and Jerry's Foundation

Authors: Joseph Kiefer and Martin Kemple
Editor: Melanie Menagh
Design: Brian Prendergast, Brian P. Graphic Arts
Illustrations: Robin Wimbiscus

ACKNOWLEDGMENTS

Digging Deeper is the culmination of 10 years of Food Works' experiences in schools and communities demonstrating how gardens can be used to grow food, grow children, and grow curriculum.

The book represents a labor of love working with hundreds of students, teachers, elders, and families from across Vermont and North America. They all have taught us so much about the lifelong wonders of learning firsthand from a garden. In this, we are deeply indebted to the Common Roots schools and community sites here in Vermont that have demonstrated such a strong commitment to integrate the story of their agricultural heritage into their school curriculum through the lessons of a garden. We feel both honored and proud to be able to share their great work with like-minded educators and youth leaders everywhere.

For the publication of the Common Roots Guidebook Series, we are grateful for the continuous support of Mima, Charlie, Jack, and Willie Tipper, whose belief in our mission working with children has been invaluable. Without them, this book would not have been possible.

Special thanks goes to Sabrina Milbury, who has been an enduring inspiration to us through her volunteer gardening work at her daughter's school down through the years, and who now joins us as a garden educator in the Food Works Master Gardening course. This book is written for all the budding Sabrinas out there, who share her passion for gardening and her commitment to growing with children.

We also extend our gratitude to the large group of wonderful and dedicated garden organizers who contributed case studies to *Digging Deeper,* including Vernon Mullins of San Antonio, Judy Elliot of Denver Urban Gardens, Lily Yeh of Philadelphia, David Hawkins of the Edible Schoolyard in Berkeley, Lisa Glick of Life Lab in Santa Cruz, Lynn Walters of Santa Fe's Cooking with Kids, Paula Hewitt of Open Road in New York City, and Gustavo Teran, who coordinates cultural exchange between the U.S. and Mexico from his home base in Vermont.

The entire staff at Food Works has been instrumental to the book's success as well: Mark Skelding, for writing the assessment and evaluation chapter; Hope Emerson, for providing crucial moral and logistical support when we needed it most; Tess Deddo, for marketing and logistics; Jude Elford, for collecting, refining, and brainstorming garden activities; Cathy Donohue for doing background research; and Todd Comen, for his invaluable insight and advice along the way. In addition, we would like to thank the Board of Directors, beginning with Dr. Bob Smilovitz, who has been a lifelong champion of community-based education for the whole child. Warm thanks also go to Board members Jim Higgins and Dr. Eleanor Ott who helped to edit this volume, and Scott Cameron and Cindy Senning for their wisdom and dedication.

Our good friends at the National Gardening Association have had an enormous influence on *Digging Deeper,* including Jim Flint, Eve Pranis, David Young, and our longtime supporter and close friend Larry Sommers.

The creativity, imagination, and dedication of our production team have been an immeasurable asset to this project. Special thanks goes to the book's designer, layout specialist, and part-time editor Brian Prendergast, whose own passion for growing flowers and foods—and children—has made him uniquely qualified to assemble, design, and refine each of the many elements of this book so beautifully. Melanie Menagh has done yeoman's work as chief editor, with help from Blake Maher and Kate Mueller. Particular acknowledgment must go to our illustrator Robin Wimbiscus, whose stunning illustrations grace each chapter of *Digging Deeper.* Libby Davidson and Matthew Sylvester also contributed valuable drawings to the book. And a grateful sigh of thanks to Kaye Alexander for shepherding the book to the printers so gracefully.

Our heartfelt love goes to our families, starting with Dolores Roy, our adopted mother who grew up in an age when gardening was second nature to families still connected to the teachings of the earth. Amy Goodman Kiefer, as our wellspring of love and support, has been a constant inspiration through her passion for plants, herbs, and wild things. And, of course, young Rachel Kemple, whose powerful imagination and boundless heart have shown us all how to follow our deepest desires.

Finally, we extend our gratitude to Karen Payne and all our friends at the American Community Gardening Association, whose social and outreach mission we share: to help grow gardens in every community across this big, beautiful land in order to restore our ties to the earth, to our food, and to one another.

To each child born of this good earth,
the elders who carry the wisdom of it,
and the teachers who nurture them all
together in a garden

FOREWORD

– by Alice Waters, Author/Chef, Chez Panisse Restaurant

About 14 years ago I moved to the house where I live now and started driving past King School on my way home from my restaurant in Berkeley, Chez Panisse, usually late at night or early in the morning. Of course, at those hours there were never any kids around, and I was troubled by what I could see from the street. The school didn't look so good. In fact, it almost looked abandoned. I would see the graffiti on the windows and the burnt-out grass, and I would wonder what had happened. Who was using this school? Who was taking care of it?

These thoughts were in the back of my mind, when one day, in an interview, I was asked about education (I was a teacher once, in a Montessori school), and I remarked on how neglected King School looked. How can this be, I asked, in an enlightened community such as Berkeley, that the public schools are allowed to deteriorate like this? No wonder, in a way, that so many parents who can afford it send their kids to private schools.

This interview appeared in print, and not long afterwards, Neil Smith, the principal of King School, called me up. He wanted to talk about what I'd said, so I invited him to lunch. It turned out we were on the same wavelength. Although we were both worried about the next generation and felt the same urgency about what was going on out there in the world, we were both optimistic about how the schools could help. And before I knew it, we were on the way to launching the Edible Schoolyard Project.

I learned that Neil, the school administration, the teachers, and the school district were all full of goodwill, willing to listen and willing to experiment with new ideas. I also learned that on the inside there were people who cared about the school. There is a beautiful courtyard garden, and a grass baseball field and a renovated auditorium where until recently the seats were held together with duct tape.

The responsibility for the physical deterioration of this school, and so many like it, lies not with the brave and underpaid teachers and administrators. Not at all. I learned that it was my responsibility, as part of a larger society that pays lip service to education but has not been willing to make it a national priority, that every child is taught as well as every other child. If we were only willing to do this—if we were all willing to take responsibility for what Jonathan Kozol has called the "savage inequalities" of American education—then we could not only turn the situation at King School around, we could renovate schools everywhere, so that the kids will know that we really care about them.

As educators from Socrates onward have recognized, the goal of education is not the mastery of various disciplines, but the mastery of one's self. Being responsible to one's self cannot be separated from being responsible to the planet. I know of no better way to get this lesson across than through a school curriculum in which food takes its place at the core level. From the garden and the kitchen and the table, you learn empathy—for each other and for all creation. You learn compassion, and you learn patience and self-discipline. A curriculum that teaches these lessons gives children an orientation to the future—and it can give them hope.

Gardening, cooking, serving and eating, composting … these are truly basic things, but the lessons they could teach are obscured and drowned out by the clamor of the media and the insidious temptations of consumerism. Kids today are bombarded with a pop culture that teaches redemption through buying things. School gardens, on the other hand, turn pop culture upside-down; they teach redemption through a deep appreciation for the real, the authentic, and the lasting—for the things that money can't buy; the very things that matter most of all if we are going to lead sane, healthy, and sustainable lives. Kids who learn environmental and nutritional lessons through school gardening and school cooking and eating—learn ethics.

Digging Deeper is an invaluable guide toward the realization of this mission.

TABLE *of* CONTENTS

A Garden in Every School,
A Center in Every Community

What do children's gardens and the fate of the planet have in common?

Answer: When they are cultivated consciously in harmony with the natural elements, then wonders that were once unimaginable emerge of their own, like a field of wildflowers suddenly appearing from under a fresh spring snow.

Growing gardens with children is a living testament to how to restore our ancient ties to the natural rhythms of the earth itself. It is in the learning of this lesson—flower by flower, child by child, season by season—that we will be able to reclaim the heritage that is rightfully ours: as the caretakers of a natural paradise where all species thrive. This is the highest aspiration for *Digging Deeper*.

There are countless reasons for young people to start a garden in their school, community, or home: to feel the power of growing their own food with their own hands; to witness the simple glory of a plant maturing from seed to flower; to work in harmony with the forces of nature as our forebears have done for centuries; to learn firsthand a wide range of basic academic skills and concepts in science, math, language arts, and social studies; to experience the satisfaction of working cooperatively with others to make the world more beautiful.

This practical, step-by-step guide for creating successful youth gardens offers all these plus one more reason for children to grow gardens where they live. Gardening provides an ideal context for youngsters, and the wider community, to reawaken their relationship to the natural world, a world that has been so transformed by human expansion in the 20th century alone. Starting with growing foods and flowers in their own neighborhoods, children can use the activities, project ideas, and resources in *Digging Deeper* to become catalysts for teaching their community a blend of life-enhancing methods for living sustainably in their own local ecosystem.

Digging Deeper will enable you to join what has become one of the fastest growing movements in North America: youth gardening. It is designed to help adults lead children in practical learning activities around food growing, nutrition education, ecological restoration, and community service learning.

For this reason, we are pleased to release *Digging Deeper* to spearhead the "Garden in Every School Campaign," which is quickly gaining momentum across the country. Initiated by the state of California in 1995, the initiative is spreading throughout the U.S. and Canada, from rural counties in Vermont and Tennessee to the cities of Denver, Pittsburgh, and Montreal. In addition to being a useful activity guide for parents and community workers, this manual is a complete tool kit for educators who want to create successful and lasting children's gardening programs as part of the "Garden in Every School Campaign."

Food Works: Grounding Education in Our Natural and Cultural Heritage

Organizing school gardening programs was our founding mission at Food Works when we first incorporated as an educational non-profit organization in Vermont in the 1980s. Having discovered what a powerful learning and organizing tool food can be in schools, we set out to help teachers, students, and parents design gardens for teaching the food growing cycle from field to table. At heart, our goal was to educate children of all ages about our ancient connection to this living earth.

We quickly realized, however, that simply growing food in schools is not enough to restore children's—and communities'—ties to the natural cycles of the earth, which we feel is so crucial for thriving on this planet into the post-industrial 21st century.

As the global economy launches headlong into the free trade telecommunications era, it has become

This has been our program focus at Food Works since the inception in 1990 of our Common Roots Program, a community-based curriculum development process for educators. Through our professional development courses, in-service workshops, and curriculum guidebook series, teachers are using youth gardens as a simple and logical starting point for developing integrated learning units that focus on students' basic needs and primary interests in their immediate environment. This work is helping to broaden the educational agendas of communities across the continent to include an ongoing process for understanding the natural and cultural heritage unique to every place, an understanding that serves as the common touchstone for every child's lifelong learning.

This process involves far more than schools and children. It includes elders to share their experience, stories, and practical wisdom; local historians, naturalists, farmers, artisans, and other professionals willing to contribute their expertise; plus homemakers, parents, families, and singles who understand the importance of cultivating a community of scholars committed to conserving and regenerating their local sense of place.

That is why we wrote this book: to deepen the collective learning process about our immediate social and natural environment far beyond the four walls of the classroom, beyond the traditional limitations of the standard subject areas, and beyond the socially prescribed boundaries between young and old, professional and amateur, expert and novice. Beginning with gardens, children can make the connections between personal nutrition, local ecology, and natural history in the context of the story of their own community. They can learn firsthand about the interrelations between their lives and the larger food, environmental, political, and economic issues of our time. And they can become competent, self-directed learners actively engaged in addressing real-life issues in their own communities.

clearer that peoples from every region and every walk of life are facing a common but historically unprecedented challenge: We must scramble to keep pace with the demands of global competition while managing to maintain our own unique identity and integrity—personally, culturally, and ecologically. The nagging question first posed by a social historian from Africa at the end of World War II seems more relevant today than ever: "How do we maintain our identity—preserve what is ours—and still achieve liberation or progress?"

We at Food Works have discovered that when people are able to address this complex issue on a local level through their educational system—including schools, businesses, civic organizations, government, churches, and outreach programs—then a strong, self-motivated generation of young learners can naturally emerge. Backed by their own community, this generation is practical and versatile enough to adapt to the changing demands of high tech society, and at the same time be culturally aware and ecologically sensitive enough to be committed to maintaining the habitability of their own region.

The Design: Planning and Implementing a Local Children's Garden Program

With this ambitious agenda providing the larger context, the following 10 chapters contain a "greenprint" for beginning and sustaining a successful youth gardening program, large or small. This includes practical tips for marshaling local resources to get started, designing an imaginative schedule of gardening activities, re-creating innovative historic theme gardens, harvesting a bounty of delicious fresh food, and organizing fun and interesting community events and projects. Special features include plans for developing food products that can be made and marketed locally, case studies of innovative youth gardening programs, and several sample curriculum activities in math, science, social studies, and language and creative arts.

Also included are:

- the do's and don'ts for identifying a garden site, mapping a garden plot, tilling the soil, and starting seeds;

- ways to meet the social and organizational challenges of launching a new project at school and in the community;

- step-by-step directions for developing a wide variety of creative garden designs;

- suggestions for how to use the local media to your advantage;

- an overview of the process for producing, packaging, and marketing local food products;

- child-tested recipes using garden-harvested foods; and

- outreach activities such as creating a Community Food Policy, conducting a watershed-wide natural resource inventory and usage plan, and transforming schools into genuine sustainable living and learning centers for all members of the community.

The essential aim of *Digging Deeper* is to cultivate the budding movement for practical, place-based education by providing a new generation of teachers, community workers, children, and parents with the fundamental tools to grow their own food safely and reliably. Together with thousands of communities around North America and the world, we see this as a crucial step toward genuine sustainability locally and human-scaled cooperation globally.

So good luck, stay in touch, and dig in!

1

First Steps

WHATEVER YOU CAN DO, OR
DREAM YOU CAN, BEGIN IT.
BOLDNESS HAS GENIUS,
POWER, AND MAGIC IN IT.

– Goethe

It was a chilly Saturday morning in early May back in the 1980s when an old FarmAll tractor rumbled down a narrow dirt road in a small but growing rural community on the outskirts of Montpelier, Vermont's capital city. The engine's roar grew louder and louder as the tractor chugged to the bottom of the hill and turned onto the blacktop. The rattling machine pulled into a circular driveway and onto a leveled, manicured lawn, ready to begin plowing.

The driver, Delmar Story, an 86-year-old former farmer, stepped off his FarmAll to survey this once-working landscape. Wearing a straw hat, flannel shirt, overalls, and work boots, Delmar chuckled quietly to himself, perhaps recalling the cornfields, cows, pigs, and chickens that were such a part of this land during his childhood. In a moment, Delmar knew just where he had to start: with the kindergarten, the Children's Garden.

It was Groundbreaking Day for this community, which was launching the first-of-its-kind educational gardening program for children, featuring a series of historic theme gardens that would bring to life the traditional foods and agricultural history of this unique place, centered on the grounds of the local school.

After Delmar had finished plowing up the kindergarten Children's Garden, he steered his tractor over to the Three Sisters Garden area, staked out in a circle. He paused for a moment, resting his weathered face on his calloused hands.

"Well, I've never plowed in a circle before," he said with a puzzled look. "But I s'pose I could try."

Reaching behind him, Delmar engaged the hydraulic lever of the plow, slowly lowered the steel blades into the soft school lawn, and began carving a circular orbit around the Three Sisters wickiup.

By then, an enthusiastic crowd of parents, teachers, children, and volunteers had gathered, and they began to clear away rocks, pile sod, rake the soil, measure walkways, stake the theme gardens, and saw up the logs for the container beds. At last, a shared dream was coming to life by their taking these first steps on a common journey specifically designed to cultivate the minds and to nurture the hearts of this community's most precious resource—its children.

The road would not be easy and the ultimate destination would remain unknown, but the next step on the journey would invariably become obvious, thanks to the commitment and determination of the original caretakers of this dream. After all, who would have guessed at the initial planning meeting—months earlier—that such a powerful outpouring of the community would eventually result in this Groundbreaking Day? Indeed, the most successful youth gardening programs become reality because of the courage and strength of the original organizers who are willing to take that first step toward the dream.

Delmar Story doing his thing.

Beginning a Youth Garden: Five Questions to Consider

To find out the demand and desire for a children's garden in your school or community, it is useful to conduct this Needs Survey of five basic questions:

1. What outdoor programs for children already exist in the community during the growing season?
2. Do any of these programs involve food, gardening, nutrition, and recreation?
3. What local organizations and individuals could help develop a youth gardening program?
4. What safe and conveniently located garden sites, with adequate sun and access to water, are available?
5. Are there sources of funding to pay for tools, seeds, compensation for the garden coordinator, and publicity?

Completing this informal Needs Survey is an important exercise. Whether you make some quick phone calls, or do a systematic survey of a broad cross-

A local farmer talks to parents and students on planting day at a school in Wardsboro, Vermont. Involving elders in youth gardens is a major factor in community building.

section of the community, this is the starting point for developing a collaborative network of people, organizations, and programs. Remember, with each conversation about the program, you are carrying the seeds of this idea onto new ground, and cultivating relationships with those people with whom you hope to be working once the program is running.

Take notes during each call. Keep a running inventory of names, phone numbers, and addresses of individuals or businesses that express an interest in becoming involved. Be sure to ask for and welcome any advice or suggestions.

Soliciting ideas from parents and community members serves several purposes. First, it's good advertising. It lets people know that there are plans for a youth garden, and that the program will reflect their input and values. Second, it can yield a list of prospective volunteers and helpers. Third, it will provide a useful database later on when you are applying for contributions from local organizations and businesses. Finally, it gives to teachers and organizers a basic blueprint of needs and goals for building the program. It describes what it is the community wants, and how a youth garden can help provide it. These findings can be announced at a press conference, or publicized on local talk-radio shows to drum up interest.

When the answers to the five questions listed here are determined, you will have the essential information you need for the first organizational meeting.

The First Organizing Meeting

Once the need for a gardening program is clearly identified, it's time to plan the first organizing meeting. Check over notes from the Needs Survey and consider everyone who's expressed an interest in the project. Who to invite to the meeting is ultimately determined by the initial organizer(s). Seek out people with any of the Four W's—Weight, Wealth, Wisdom, and Work.

- **Weight.** Contact those who have influence in the community—a political sort, a prominent business person, or a longtime resident or elder.
- **Wealth.** Wealthy members can donate to the project, and often have a network of friends and associates from whom you can solicit contributions.
- **Wisdom.** People with wisdom and experience are always important to have on board, especially in the early stages.

Sample Agenda for First Program Organizing Meeting

This list is a template into which you can fit your particular needs. Naturally, you can adapt the format to best suit your group.

PRELIMINARIES

This meeting can be hosted by a local church, school, or civic organization. At the meeting site, have name tags and refreshments laid out at the beginning—food always helps get things going. Other materials to have on hand:

- pens and paper
- markers
- a flip chart (important)
- masking tape
- a pad of paper to pass around for people's names, organizations, phone numbers, e-mail addresses, etc.

If most people attending don't know one another already, someone with good organizational skills who can stimulate lively, focused discussion should act as a facilitator. The facilitator should be chosen ahead of time so he or she can prepare.

THE MEETING CAN PROCEED AS FOLLOWS:

1. **Welcome** by organizer(s) or facilitator.
2. **Purpose** of meeting and agenda review.
3. **Introductions**. Attendees give name, organization, programs, and population served.
4. **History**. Outline the process so far, presenting a strong, clear vision of the project. Show the results of the Needs Survey. Use slides or other visuals if available.
5. **Future Vision**. Discuss the larger, far-reaching aspirations of a youth gardening program. Find out how many people would be willing to assist in creating such a project, and what they feel its major goals should be. Use the flip chart to record ideas.
6. **Getting Started**. Discuss what needs to be done to get started. Draw up a list of tasks to be accomplished—locating a site, obtaining materials, publicity and outreach, developing program activities, etc.
7. **Forming Committees**. Decide what committees are needed to divide up the list of tasks efficiently. Consider the following committees:
- *Coordinating*. Organizes and oversees general operations. Members should have the most available time and energy. A core coordinating committee assumes the responsibility for overall operations of the program. The members may change over time, but to insure continuity, a strong, dedicated coordinating committee is key.
- *Program*. Organizes day-to-day activities of the project.
- *Fundraising*. Solicits contributions. In addition to cash, contributions also include donations of materials and services such as tools, seeds, and advertising.
- *Publicity and Outreach*. Develops printed materials, arranges community events, and contacts media outlets.
8. **Assigning Tasks**. Ask for volunteers for each committee, then allow the committees 15 minutes to work together to discuss the committee's purpose and to define each person's duties.
9. **Review**. The whole group should then review each committee's discussion. On the flip chart, record each committee's priorities and tasks.
10. **Set a Date for the Next Meeting**. Identify a facilitator. Review specific tasks for each committee to complete by the next meeting.

❧ **Work.** It is essential to have people who will roll up their sleeves and take on the major tasks and responsibilities of the project.

To get input from potential participants, invite a few highly motivated local kids who would be directly affected by a youth gardening initiative.

Keep in mind that this first "organizing meeting" could very well consist of a single teacher and a telephone. In this case, the responsibilities outlined in the meeting agenda on page 5 can be streamlined. Choose the essential tasks that can be reasonably performed by those people working on the project at the time. The other jobs can be delegated once momentum begins to build.

In the best-case scenario, when a group of volunteers is available to lay the groundwork, the agenda on page 5 can be used for the first organizing meeting. Afterwards, send a follow-up thank-you letter to all participants. This should include the minutes of the meeting, a list of the committees formed and their tasks, and the time, location, and agenda of the next meeting. If there is a very small turnout at the first meeting, the smaller group can form the Coordinating Committee. Start a binder and save materials to document the process for future reference.

Three Key Areas for Program Promotion

After a group of volunteers has met and discussed the nature and direction of the project, the next step is to enlist the cooperation of as many people and organizations as possible.

Seeking Youth Participation

The primary audience for a youth gardening program is children and their families. While the need for such a program may be established by a Needs Survey, this is no guarantee that children will participate.

Involving the school is essential to success. School grounds can be used for the gardens, teachers are usually very enthusiastic about incorporating gardening into their curriculum, and many of the children who help plant the garden in springtime tend to continue on in the summer program. When school resumes in the fall, teachers can introduce activities around the harvest, so the garden learning experience extends through the seasons and across the curriculum. (See Chapter Eight for a more complete guide on school gardening curriculum development.)

You can also circulate flyers in the local schools— with the principals' permission—announcing the program. Include a tear-off registration form to be filled out and returned to the school or to your organization's address. Other means for reaching the student population include contacting existing recreation programs, the YMCA or YWCA, libraries, churches, and arts programs.

Building In-Kind and Volunteer Support

The local business community is a second important area for program promotion. Businesses need to understand the advantages of being connected to a gardening program. Make a clear, cogent case for how the participation of a business will benefit local people—their customers. Businesses can also be encouraged to donate materials; this way they can contribute without major outlays of cash.

❧ **In-kind Contributions:** The local hardware store may be tapped for shovels and trowels; the nursery for seeds, potting soil, and seed trays; the lumber yard for wood, nails, and building materials. Draw up a list of materials, then present it to businesses to see what they wish to contribute.

❧ **Volunteer Day:** Hold a community Volunteer Day on a Saturday morning. Advertise through newspapers, radio, TV, fliers, and posters. Invite people to come to the garden site to pick up litter, build garden beds, hoe rows, plant seeds, and carry water. Supply refreshments and call on volunteers for long-term service.

❧ **Americorps:** Americorps volunteers can be enlisted for much of the difficult, often tedious, groundwork necessary for launching a community project.

Raising Awareness and Educating the Community

Although designed primarily to serve participating children, youth gardening also provides an excellent opportunity to educate the general public about food and nutrition issues through radio interviews, newspaper articles, and TV coverage.

Work with a local newspaper to promote daily and weekly garden activities in the calendar-of-events section. Create a weekly news column updating the community on your progress. For the garden groundbreaking ceremony, send out a press release well in advance and invite local church, civic, and political representatives. Arrange your gardening calendar to ensure that there is a press-worthy event every week. The local press can cover events such as the ground-breaking/seed-planting ceremony, a food drive or donations from the garden to a local food shelf, a theater and arts ceremony, first-harvest celebration, community-wide meals at the garden, donations from area businesses, etc.

Pick a catchy name and logo. Choose a name that defines your project and gives it a local flavor. Once you settle on a name, use it to identify yourselves whenever possible so that it stays in people's minds as a project worth supporting. Here is a sampling of names from other projects: The Lettuce Eat Garden, The Newport Roots Garden, The Barre City Three Sisters Garden.

Produce a broadsheet or newsletter with the logo prominently displayed. This is a communications tool, informing the Organizing Committee and wider community of the program's progress. The newsletter can include pictures and articles by the children, advertisements, a list of contributors, contests and puzzles, interviews, photos, and letters to the editor.

Fundraising

Beyond in-kind donations and volunteer support, a children's gardening program needs financial backing. Fundraising is a crucial aspect of any outreach mission. Soliciting money to support youth gardening should not be seen as begging for handouts, but rather as enlisting people's help in a unique, exciting project that will benefit the entire community.

Fundraising Events

Fundraising events can be held around the garden. The Volunteer Day described can be combined with a fundraiser, offering baked goods, home-cooked foods, and household items. Raise money with a pot-luck feast and dance.

When harvesting begins, flowers, vegetables, and herbs can be sold to raise money. Be sure to keep your organizing committee apprised of fundraising opportunities throughout the gardening season.

Grant Writing

Begin your fundraising efforts by writing a funding grant to a local bank, business, or service organization. Choose one and call its community relations director. Explain the project, and mention a few people on your organizing committee—weight and

wealth are important here. Request a grant application form.

Work with your coordinating committee to draft a winning grant application geared to fund a specific part of the project, such as the program coordinator's salary, tools, advertising, etc.

On the national scene, a great place to look for start-up materials is the National Gardening Association's Youth Gardening Grants Program. Dozens of children's gardening projects have been launched by the NGA's in-kind contributions of tools, seeds, and other essentials needed for getting started. For an application, write: The National Gardening Association, 180 Flynn Avenue, Burlington, Vermont 05401.

Above all, persevere. Raising money to start up a new project can be one of the biggest bugaboos for first-time organizers. Skepticism can be high, competition fierce, and generosity stretched to the limit, given the barrage of solicitations a typical business or average householder receives in a given week. But a clear commitment by the project coordinators to make youth gardens a permanent fixture in the community—combined with solid backing from a dedicated Organizing Committee—will invariably lay a strong foundation for ongoing support over the long term.

Children in detention custody making raised bed gardens at the Porter Leath Children's Center in Memphis, Tennessee. This project was kicked off by an in-kind grant from the National Gardening Association's Youth Gardening Grants Program. Garden coordinator Laurie Williams said, "I would recommend that anyone trying to start a program apply for the NGA's Youth Gardening Grant. They provided us with hoes, rakes, sprinklers, books, a rain gauge—so much of what we needed to get up and running."

San Antonio and Vernon Mullens— Leading the Way to a Sustainable Future

If any city in the country can boast of being the "Youth Garden Capital of America," it is San Antonio, Texas. Back in 1990, the San Antonio Independent School District, in partnership with the Bexar County Master Gardeners Program, made a commitment to establish eight new gardens every fall at inner-city schools. By 1995, over 10,000 San Antonio students were actively involved in gardening programs, and 300 community volunteers were contributing more than 21,000 hours of community service per year to gardening with children. In 1998, 192 San Antonio Schools from 15 school districts have subscribed to and implemented a gardening program with the ongoing assistance of the Texas Agricultural Extension Service at Texas A&M.

If any community member can lay claim to being among the most dedicated youth garden volunteers in America, it is San Antonio's Master Gardener, Vernon Mullens. "The Gray Gardener" has made the crucial link between community growing and school gardening by leading classes for area schoolchildren in his own small community garden plot, with subject areas ranging from herbology to nutrition to social studies. He has also developed garden-based curriculum with teachers to take back to their schoolyards and classrooms.

"Down here we like to think of ourselves as a big gardening family," says Mullens. "I guess the common bond of our program is our love for gardening. That's what keeps our programs on the leading edge of master gardening."

The list of theme gardens he has pioneered in San Antonio is testimony to the imagination and passion of this man who volunteers over 600 hours of community service a year to teach children about the age-old wisdom gained from working the land. The "Brains and Grains Garden" produces six different kinds of traditional grains, including amaranth, millet, and maize, introducing children "to some of the ancient secrets of human cultures, history, and horticulture," says Mullens.

The popular "Dietcise Garden" includes a nutritional and medicinal guide of common (and uncommon) vegetables, along with planting schemes for growing veggies that are especially good for treating medical conditions such as diabetes—plant beans and peas together with grains to provide complete proteins.

The "Melting Pot Garden" combines foods from San Antonio's diverse ethnic communities—Hispanic, African-American, Asian, and Native American—together with a study unit on the cultural and geographic origins of garden vegetables, using world maps, atlases, and resource reference books.

Vernon Mullens' growing success, however, is not solely due to his own determination and commitment. It is part of a larger countywide classroom garden program that is a national model for integrating food growing into the heart of school curriculum. The model draws from a coordinated community volunteer campaign through the Bexar County Master Garden program. Headed by Master Gardener Calvin Finch through the Texas Agricultural Extension Service, the Classroom Garden Program offers teachers three hours of basic training in horticulture education, a packet of curriculum materials, supplies for building raised beds, garden soil, fertilizer, seeds, and transplants every fall and spring, three hours of continuing

> *Begin now to study the little things in your own dooryard.*
>
> – *Dr. George Washington Carver, from the curriculum materials of Master Gardener Vernon Mullens, San Antonio*

education every fall and spring, plus expert Master Gardeners on call to provide advice throughout the growing season. All this, for a one-time fee of $250.

Together with other great youth garden cities like Pittsburgh, Denver, San Francisco, and Seattle, San Antonio and Vernon Mullens are at the forefront of a growing national movement to revitalize neighborhoods and restore communities through local food growing and ecological stewardship, beginning with children.

ABOVE: *Vernon Mullens teaching at the San Jacinto Teaching Arbor, San Antonio.* BELOW: *A team of second graders at an intergenerational garden in San Antonio.*

2

Developing a Program Plan

The organizational groundwork for beginning a youth gardening program is now laid: the core questions and basic principles are outlined; the first organizing meeting has been held; the coordinating committee is chosen; and plans for garnering local support are underway, including fundraising activities.

It is now time to design a day-to-day program that will inspire children and the entire community. This chapter includes an outline of daily activities, a weekly schedule, and a sample eight-week program of garden themes and projects for children.

Start Small and Work with a Team

When the program reaches the planning stages, enthusiasm may be running high and proposals may be afoot to develop a full-year children's gardening project. Experience has shown, however, that it is best to start small for a first-time program.

The first year a modest, but successful, garden will yield a richer harvest of food and learning experiences than a large, over-ambitious program that doesn't receive the proper care and nourishment. Even a small plot can be transformed into an interesting, unusual garden habitat that children will be proud of, and that the community will want to continue to support.

Every community has a diversity of gardening talent and skills waiting to be utilized. Even two people can make a team, and a small group of people working together can move mountains.

There are many reasons why the team approach works better than having one person doing it all. Here are a half dozen important ones:

Six Reasons for Building a Garden Team

1. It can be difficult to work in isolation with no constructive feedback for your ideas and programs.
2. A garden can encompass many different needs and interests—nutrition education, horticulture, arts and crafts, and intergenerational learning. Few people are capable of teaching all these skills well.
3. Many hands make light work.
4. The power that grows from diversity is mirrored in the life of a garden.
5. The many demands of youth gardening are best served by a group that gives and receives support, counsel, advice, and encouragement.
6. Working with others is more ecologically sound than working alone. Teamwork demonstrates to the children alternatives to competition and the value of working together toward a shared goal.

Enlisting Local Talent for Your Team

Whether you are in a rural, suburban, or urban community, there are many volunteers whose help is only a phone call away. The best place to start is your Organizing Committee. If you have chosen a group well equipped with the Four W's, committee members should have a network of contacts.

Next, review the Needs Survey on page 4, and match program needs to available resources. Make a list of who's who in horticulture, craft-making, landscaping, childcare, etc. Draw out hidden local talent, people who would like to share their wealth of knowledge and experience with children. Compile a master list of likely candidates from all these sources.

The next step is to call people on the master list to ask if they would like to volunteer. People respond when they are asked. Invite the ones who express an interest to an organizational tea to discuss the garden program.

At the meeting, find out which activities each person might like to offer. Talk about a calendar of events to set up daily activities, a weekly schedule, and a summer-long program.

Having a crackerjack team makes any project run more smoothly and successfully. The chart below shows ways to help insure success. Through this process, two types of teams generally emerge:

❧ **The All-Weather Team:** These are the people who are ready to commit to the effort through thick and thin. Include them in as many aspects of the planning and implementation process as possible.

❧ **The Fair-Weather Team:** If you are basically running the show yourself, you are the program team. You should, however, enlist a wider group of parents, elders, farmers, gardeners, etc., who you initially contacted when setting up the program. While this is not a formal team, it is important to include people as partners working toward the same goal. Find the best way for each of them to become involved so that they feel valued.

Planning an Effective Gardening and Activities Schedule

Planning a schedule of seasonal themes and activities for a children's gardening program is as important as planning the vegetables, herbs, and flowers to be planted.

In the northern part of the country, for example, avid gardeners often spend long winter nights browsing through seed catalogs and gardening magazines, envisioning the plant varieties, planting strategies, and garden designs for the coming season. This process sets a calendar for the whole growing season— when to start seedlings, when and where to transplant, what to harvest at which times over the season, and how, when, and what foods to preserve in the fall.

This same kind of long-range planning is essential for creating a week-by-week, day-by-day gardening program for children. A methodical, well-thought-out schedule provides a reliable framework for the leadership team and the children, guiding the flow of activities throughout the course of the program.

Keep in mind that all the activity suggestions outlined here are just that—ideas that should be modified according to your specific needs, interests, and capacities. The uniqueness of each locale will determine the exact garden designs, horticulture activities, arts and recreation projects, and community-wide celebrations for each program.

The outcome of any project connected to nature is impossible to control or predict. Just as no two gardens are the same, no two garden programs will be the same. The unique ecology of each place means that the geography, growing season, soil, birds, and insects, as well as the regional history, traditional knowledge, and local lore, will all be different and unique. For example, the feeling one gets of the land in Vermont contrasts sharply with that of the Pacific

Five Keys for Effective Team Building

1. Communication. This includes learning the skills of active listening, conflict resolution, and simple trust among group members. Effective communication is the most crucial component of team building.

2. Goals. Present a clear, simple outline of how a garden program will benefit not just children, but the entire community.

3. Roles. Identify the skills and talents of your team, their roles and schedules, and the tasks they are to perform.

4. Timeline. Create a calendar specifying weekly themes and activities; include a detailed plan of action for each person.

5. Ongoing assessment. The weekly routine should include a process for updating and evaluating the program, as well as team member activities, challenges, and interpersonal issues and concerns.

Needs-Based Garden Design

NEEDS	GARDEN DESIGN OPPORTUNITIES	SAMPLE PROGRAM IDEAS
Nutrition Education	Outdoor nutrition center—Nutrition café, nutritional education resources Solar food dryer, solar ovens Each garden area with a central circular sitting area for hands-on lessons in nutrition education Central courtyard—a multi-use space for festivals, community gatherings, and a place to discuss proper nutrition and how to grow food for a healthy diet	Cooking and baking activities using the Food Guide Pyramid (page 64) Cultural and ethnic cooking
Basic Horticulture	Sitting place to observe and document food, flower and herb growth built into each garden design Outdoor work table for transplanting and seed starting Seats, benches made of logs, or large stones Wide and well-mulched walkways Creative ecological planting of each garden—interplanting of vegetables, flowers, herbs, and habitats for beneficial insects, birds, frogs Bird houses, compost system, beneficial insect habitats Tool shed	Learning across the curriculum in sciences (life science, earth science), math (measurement, plant growth, weight, height); language arts (journal writing, poetry, descriptive observation); creative arts (drawings, paintings) Daily class on garden ecology for understanding the life cycle of plants, soil science
Building Community	Garden Courtyards—intergenerational gathering place for face-to-face communication Community Bulletin Board—events calendar, garden jobs to be done, notices, information exchange, job wheel Fences—a fence can either attract or repel vandalism, but if done artfully with plants and vines growing up, a fence can provide both respect and safety for the garden	Storytelling with elders and farmers Intergenerational classes Performances by children Festivals and celebrations of place—planting ceremony, midsummer garden festival, harvest dinners
Creative Arts	Murals, banners, flags Adventure playground where kids feel a sense of ownership Performing arts area Signage Maps	Creative arts program Garden drama—skits, costumes Student-made signs for compost station, courtyard, birdhouses, research area for cover crops, etc. Press plants Draw and identify plant parts (page 59)
Entrepreneurial Opportunities	Market stand with roof and shelves for displaying produce Develop a specialty food product (see page 52)	Basic math skills—cash sales, accounting, bookkeeping Market research on cost of locally grown organic food to determine prices
Community Service Learning	Emergency food shelf garden	Designate a special area of the garden for donations Donate harvest to a local food shelf

Northwest coastline or the cornbelt of Iowa. Gardening challenges us to invent new ways of relating to the surrounding natural world by creating imaginative designs that reflect the local climate, landscape, flora, and fauna.

Likewise, program themes should vary based on the needs and ages of the participants, as well as the garden's own stage of development. The programs suggested here are samples intended to provide the basic ideas for constructing a program tailored to each community's particular needs.

For instance, a first-year garden requires a lot of time building the garden's infrastructure—the walkways, compost, birdhouses, etc. An established garden program might focus more on experimenting with new kinds of vegetables and herbs. Similarly, themes and activities designed for rural Vermont kindergarteners will not work for a group of junior high students in San Antonio. The age and interests of program participants are as important to consider when selecting themes and activities as are the history and climate of your area.

Following are activity ideas and themes for sample day, week, and eight-week garden programs.

A SAMPLE DAY IN THE GARDEN

9:00–9:30 AM

Opening Circle in Courtyard
- Small snack—*mint-flavored tea and quartered peanut butter and jelly sandwiches with apple slices*
- Story/Song/Puppet Show
- Personal check-in: Use a talking stick to give each child a chance to speak
- Portfolios update: What has been accomplished?
- Review the day's schedule

9:30–10:00 AM

Garden Discovery
- Children record garden observations in journal and share with the group
- Team-building activity: Trust Circle

10:00–10:30 AM

Horticultural Education
- Companion planting, thinning carrots

10:30–11:00 AM

Garden Job Wheel
- Mulching, composting, thinning, planting, record keeping, harvesting

11:00–11:15 AM BREAK

11:15 AM–12:15 PM

Nutrition Education and Culinary Arts
- Nutritional garden salad bar
- Group nutrition lesson: Constructing a Food Guide Pyramid from locally made and processed foods
- Food preparation: Guest chef from senior center
- Optional daily cooking class

12:15–12:45 PM LUNCH

12:45–1:45 PM

Garden Choice Activity Time
- Arts and crafts: Making garden ecology bags, plant press, mask making, thank-you cards, puppet show, garden games
- Building projects in the garden: Birdhouses, sign making, wooden seats, plant presses
- Journal writing

1:45–2:00 PM
CLOSING CIRCLE

A SAMPLE WEEK IN THE GARDEN

MONDAY

9:00 Morning Circle:
Review, stories, snack

9:30 Garden Discovery:
Observation time in the
garden

10:00 Horticultural Ed.:
What is a weed? Why
weed?

10:30 Job Wheel

11:00 Free Time, Break

11:15 Nutrition Ed.
and Culinary Arts

12:15 Lunch and Free Play

12:45 Garden Activities

1:45 Closing Circle

TUESDAY

9:00 Morning Circle

9:30 Garden Discovery

10:00 Horticultural Ed.:
Weed identification

10:30 Job Wheel

11:00 Free Time, Break

11:15 Nutrition Ed.
and Culinary Arts

12:15 Lunch and Free Play

12:45 Creative Arts: Masks,
painting, murals, signs

1:45 Closing Circle

WEDNESDAY

9:00 Field Trip: Food shelf,
farm, or food store

12:00 Harvest Food

12:15 Lunch and Free Play

12:45 Performance Practice

1:45 Closing Circle

THURSDAY

9:00 Morning Circle

9:30 Garden Discovery

10:00 Horticultural Ed.: Which
weeds grow where? Which
weeds are edible?

10:30 Job Wheel

11:00 Free Time, Break

11:15 Nutrition Ed.
and Culinary Arts

12:15 Lunch and Free Play

12:45 Community Service:
Flower-planting in the park

1:45 Closing Circle

FRIDAY

9:00 Morning Circle

9:30 Garden Discovery

10:00 Horticultural Ed.: How
many weeds in our garden
can we identify and draw?

10:30 Job Wheel

11:00 Free Time, Break

11:15 Nutrition Ed.
and Culinary Arts

12:15 Lunch with parents and
friends

12:45 Garden Matinee:
*The Case of the Mystery
Weed: Friend or Foe?*

2:00 Applause and Thank Yous

A Sample Eight-Week Garden Activities Program

When scheduling activities for a youth garden program, come up with a list of weekly themes well in advance. Ideally, these themes should follow the natural growing cycle of the garden and match the specific developmental needs of the children in your group.

Four Components of a Weekly Theme

1. Choose themes that suggest a variety of imaginative, creative learning opportunities for children, families, and the community at large. Listed below are numerous possible themes that lend themselves to a multitude of hands-on activities for children of all ages.

A SAMPLE EIGHT-WEEK CYCLE IN THE GARDEN

WEEK ONE:

THEME:
Growing in nature's garden.

DISCOVERY QUESTIONS:
How does our food grow?
Why grow our own food?

VEGETABLE OF THE WEEK:
Lettuce.

HORTICULTURE ACTIVITIES:
Five-Senses Attunement Exercise.
Plant seeds, transplant seedlings.
Identify garden research areas.
Insect i.d. Weed i.d. Vegetable
observation. Weather.

CREATIVE GARDEN ARTS:
Nature's food web theater, masks.
Map your garden and identify.
Press lettuce leaves.
Begin vegetable portfolio.

NUTRITION:
Nature's food chain: What is the
food web in nature's garden?
Stake out and create
Nutrition Café area.
Paper plate meal design.
Start daily nutrition diary.
Rhubarb pie recipe.

INTERGENERATIONAL:
Heirloom lettuce varieties, story.

**COMMUNITY GIVING &
ENTREPRENEURIAL:**
Lettuce container gifts.
Sell mesculin salad mix.

LOCAL RESOURCE PERSON:
Farmer, naturalist.

WEEK TWO:

THEME:
Soil.

DISCOVERY QUESTIONS:
How does soil help plants grow?
How do we feed our soil?

VEGETABLE OF THE WEEK:
Carrots.

HORTICULTURE ACTIVITIES:
Make your own seedling soil.
Compost-in-a-baggy experiments.
Conduct pH and NPK soil tests.
Layer a compost pile.
Grass clipping soil mulch.
Plant a cover crop.

CREATIVE GARDEN ARTS:
Sketch a square-foot soil profile
and create a compost collage.
Make compost signs.
Soil Mystery Theater.

NUTRITION:
Introduction to the Food Guide
Pyramid. Continue daily nutrition
diary. Vegetable vitamins.
Shredded carrot and lettuce salad.

INTERGENERATIONAL:
Storytelling.
Carrot experiences—meals,
recipes, storage.

**COMMUNITY GIVING &
ENTREPRENEURIAL:**
Start an earthworm farm as a gift for
a local childcare center.

LOCAL RESOURCE PERSON:
Farmer, cooperative extension agent,
agronomist.

WEEK THREE:

THEME:
Seeds and Propagation.

DISCOVERY QUESTIONS:
How do seeds grow in the soil?
How do we grow seedlings to
transplant outdoors?

VEGETABLE OF THE WEEK:
Beans, squash, corn.
Three Sisters Garden.

HORTICULTURE ACTIVITIES:
Parts of a seed.
Seed germination experiment.
Making sprouts. Thinning.

GARDEN RESEARCH:
Vegetable survival diagnosis.
What's growing and what's not?
Wild seed research and saving.

CREATIVE GARDEN ARTS:
Seed collage. Three Sisters Garden
Theater. Seed necklaces.

NUTRITION:
Preserve dilly beans.
Vegetarian Food Guide Pyramid.
Edible seeds and snacks.
Grind wheat berries.
Make bread, three-bean salad, and
sprouted bean and seed salad.
Continue daily nutrition diary.

INTERGENERATIONAL:
Storytelling, bean recipes.

**COMMUNITY GIVING &
ENTREPRENEURIAL:**
Build a solar oven.

LOCAL RESOURCE PERSON:
Farmer, nursery manager.

2. Plan weekly themes that follow the natural rhythm of the garden itself, from planting to harvest.
3. Provide links from one theme to the next, so that the program grows from week to week, building awareness, understanding, and appreciation of natural cycles.
4. For each theme, focus on ways of linking community skills and expertise to the garden, including areas such as horticultural experience, recipes, and family stories.

WEEK FOUR:

THEME:
Botany.

DISCOVERY QUESTIONS:
How do plants grow in the garden? What are the different parts of plants, and how do they make seeds?

VEGETABLE OF THE WEEK:
Tomato.

HORTICULTURE ACTIVITIES:
Identify roots, stems, flowers, buds, leaves. Flower dissection. Seed-plant cycle. Saving tomato seeds.

CREATIVE GARDEN ARTS:
Make a clay-toothpick flower. Plant-parts mural. Botany Theater. Tomato leaf press.

NUTRITION:
Plant-parts soup or salad. Continue daily nutrition diary. Tomato sauce and English muffin pizzas, green tomato pie, salsa recipes, "plant-parts salad" recipe.

INTERGENERATIONAL:
Storytelling, recipes, tomato drying, freezing, and canning techniques.

COMMUNITY GIVING & ENTREPRENEURIAL:
Give a "plant-part salad" gift to a senior center.

LOCAL RESOURCE PERSON:
Farmer, botanist, naturalist.

WEEK FIVE:

THEME:
Flowers and Herbs.

DISCOVERY QUESTIONS:
What flowers and herbs can we grow in our garden? How can we use them?

VEGETABLE OF THE WEEK:
Basil and Marigold.

HORTICULTURE ACTIVITIES:
Role of flowers and herbs. Culinary and medicinal herbs. Insect-repelling flowers. Wildflower identification. Flower arranging. Dry and serve basil.

CREATIVE GARDEN ARTS:
Flower and herb press. The story of "Miss Rumphius." Flower gift cards.

NUTRITION:
Continue daily nutrition diary. Make herbal tea mix and bags from chamomile, lemon balm, spearmint. Edible flowers.

INTERGENERATIONAL:
Storytelling, flower arranging.

COMMUNITY GIVING & ENTREPRENEURIAL:
Make a label, and sell dry basil and mint tea. Donate flowers to local hospital.

LOCAL RESOURCE PERSON:
Farmer, florist, herbalist.

INTERGENERATIONAL:
Storytelling, recipes.

COMMUNITY GIVING & ENTREPRENEURIAL:
Give local insect i.d. to school library. Yarrow sale—beneficial insect plants.

LOCAL RESOURCE PERSON:
Farmer, entomologist.

WEEK SEVEN:

THEME:
Harvest and Food Preservation.

DISCOVERY QUESTION:
What can we do with our harvest?

VEGETABLE OF THE WEEK:
Onion.

HORTICULTURE ACTIVITIES:
Food preservation techniques—canning, freezing, drying.
Food storage locations—pantries, root cellars, freezers.
Plant cover crop.
Braiding onions for storage.

CREATIVE GARDEN ARTS:
Make food preservation labels.
Local recipe book.
Make cover for plant press portfolio.

NUTRITION:
Chips (from corn meal) and salsa.

INTERGENERATIONAL:
Storytelling, recipes, putting food by stories.

COMMUNITY GIVING & ENTREPRENEURIAL:
Sell salsa and other harvested veggies, donate to food shelf, storytelling at local childcare center.

LOCAL RESOURCE PERSON:
Farmer, chef.

WEEK SIX:

THEME:
Insects.

DISCOVERY QUESTION:
What insects are in our garden and what do they do there?

VEGETABLE OF THE WEEK:
Broccoli.

HORTICULTURE ACTIVITIES:
Insect i.d. Predator-prey relationships and parasitoids. Beneficial habitats (umbels—dill, yarrow). Natural insect controls (ground-up cayenne, soap suds, and water spray).

CREATIVE GARDEN ARTS:
Make insect masks for Insect Detectives Theater.

NUTRITION:
Continue daily nutrition diary.
Freezing broccoli, stir-fry, broccoli with dip.

WEEK EIGHT:

THEME:
Community Celebration.

DISCOVERY QUESTION:
How do we celebrate our garden harvest with others?

VEGETABLE OF THE WEEK:
Zucchini.

HORTICULTURE ACTIVITIES:
Making local food products (salsa, pizza, pickles, dilly beans, pesto, tea bags, jams).
Mulching and putting garden to bed. Cover cropping. Compost.

CREATIVE GARDEN ARTS:
Creative table settings and artistic menu. Create favors using local herbs and flowers.
Garden Harvest Theater presentation to community—poetry, songs, skits, awards, diary reading.

NUTRITION:
Culminating menu and meal.
Paper plate post-test (with Food Guide Pyramid).
Zucchini bread, zucchini stir-fry, pesto, herbal vinaigrette.

INTERGENERATIONAL:
Stories of harvest celebrations and helping others from yesteryear.

COMMUNITY GIVING & ENTREPRENEURIAL:
Host a community Giving Meal.
Plant product sale.

LOCAL RESOURCE PERSON:
Farmer, civic organization leader, sponsoring business, local food product person.

It Takes a Village

Most people who know the tough turf of North Philadelphia would hardly expect to find it home to an award-winning garden. With a reputation for having fallen prey to urban as well as botanic blight, North Philadelphia has had neighborhoods better known for abandoned lots than for lush greenery.

That's all changed with The Village of Arts and Humanities, an aggregation of buildings, parks, and gardens devoted to the cultural and spiritual enrichment of its neighbors—especially children. In 1986, artist Lily Yeh joined forces with residents, enlisting local kids to clear a trash-filled lot and build a place where art and nature would coexist. From that initial effort, the Village currently encompasses eight community parks and gardens, along with four formerly abandoned buildings that are now being used for community education and arts activities.

The aim of the Village program is to integrate the arts with live, growing things. The vegetable and flower gardens are complemented by sculptures, murals, and mosaics designed and executed by children. A Chinese garden sits among African-American sculptures in a multi-cultural symbiosis.

Each year there are garden festivals celebrating the summer's achievements. In 1996, the Village's vegetable garden won first prize in the City Garden Contest sponsored by the Pennsylvania Horticultural Society.

Lily Yeh has taken the Village garden spirit international, transforming a barren churchyard in Korogocho, Kenya, into a flower garden decorated with bright angels. The education program in Philadelphia, meanwhile, incorporates the study of world cultures through food, including the growing of grains from different regions around the globe in Philadelphia's neighborhood gardens. The longevity and diversity of The Village of Arts and Humanities are a testimony to the power of the arts in kindling the spirit of community and restoring our ties to the earth.

Garden theater, ritual, music, and dance are not merely interesting spectacles for entertaining the community. They are the very stuff that a community's culture is made of. The best children's gardening programs don't try to fit "the arts" into a pre-established agenda, but instead cultivate project ideas, garden designs, and horticultural activities based on the natural creative instincts and artistic passion of the children themselves, young and old.

3

CHAPTER THREE

Garden Design Ideas

GOD ALMIGHTY FIRST

PLANTED A GARDEN.

– Francis Bacon,
Of Gardens

This chapter includes step-by-step instructions for creating five different types of gardens with children: a straight-row Heritage Garden, a Three Sisters Garden, a Vitamin A Nutrition Garden, a Pizza Garden, and a Community Mosaic Garden. Brief descriptions of a number of other garden designs are also included, as well as an activity plan for creating a locally grown specialty food product using vegetables cultivated by children.

Getting started with the Heritage Garden

The simplest and most practical way to get started in gardening is to draw on the horticultural knowledge and experience that already exist locally. The Heritage Garden is a natural first choice because it is based on the gardening techniques and vegetables, herbs, and flowers that families have used in the community over many generations. Indeed, most backyard gardens in the U.S. are characteristic of the Heritage Garden.

The Heritage Garden is typically laid out as a flat garden in straight rows, with two- to three-foot walkways in between. The annual vegetables usually grown in a Heritage Garden include lettuces, carrots, beats, onions, tomatoes, peppers, beans, and peas. Vegetables unique to the various regional ethnic groups can also be cultivated. For example, neighborhoods with a large Chinese population will often have gardens with bok choy, totsoi, and Chinese cabbage; Italian communities will typically have gardens that include tomatoes, basil, onion, and garlic.

In well-drained garden soil, the major advantages of a Heritage Garden are that children can plant, weed, mulch, and transplant with relative ease. The downside of this garden is that it requires more space than one using intensive gardening techniques. Raised-bed gardens, for example, can grow the same amount of vegetables in a much smaller space.

The Heritage Garden: Step-by-Step

Making a straight-row Heritage Garden is a very simple process.

1. Plow the site thoroughly using a rototiller, plow, or hand tools.
2. After removing all large clods of roots, weeds, and other debris, put stakes in each of the four corners of the garden plot.
3. On a scale map, plan out the garden rows, specifying what is to be grown in each row.
4. According to your garden plan from Step 3, put stakes on either end of the garden rows.

The straight-row garden is the classic American garden.

5. Run string between the stakes. This designates the rows where the vegetables will be planted.
6. Plant following the line of the strings.
7. Try putting straw or mulch on either side of the planted rows to prevent weeds or other undesirable plants from taking root.
8. As an extension, cordon off small areas for compost, birdhouses, and a birdbath. Consider a small sitting area for observation, reflection, and relaxation.

Working with Local Resources

The beauty of the Heritage Garden is that it can be a wonderful link to share and celebrate the unique cultural mix of each community. The Heritage Garden provides an ideal opportunity to invite elders to share their knowledge and experience, as well as their heirloom seeds and older varieties of vegetables and flowers. Do some local research and discover ways of involving residents of diverse cultures in growing different foods that reflect their roots.

The Three Sisters Garden

Growing a traditional Native American garden is a good way to establish a close connection to the first human settlers in any region. The Three Sisters Garden, consisting of corn, beans, and squash, is a relatively simple garden that has been grown by Native Americans for centuries. This garden is planted in a ring, symbolizing the unending cycle of life, death, and rebirth. The garden consists of two concentric circles, one approximately five feet and the other 15 feet in diameter.

For a collection of fun activities, great stories, and creative design ideas, consult the book *In The Three Sisters Garden*, Common Roots Press, (802) 223-1515.

The Three Sisters Garden: Step-by-Step

1. Mark a circular area 15 feet in diameter and till the entire circle.
2. Mark an inner circle of five feet in diameter in the center of the larger circle. This can be used as a special sitting spot in the middle for quiet contemplation and storytelling.

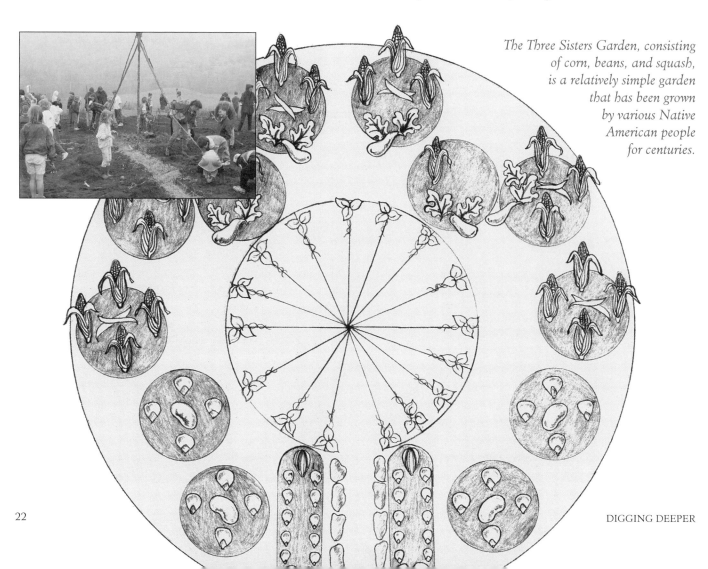

The Three Sisters Garden, consisting of corn, beans, and squash, is a relatively simple garden that has been grown by various Native American people for centuries.

3. Mark and establish walkways running north-south and east-west, honoring the four directions.

4. Gather 10 to 20 poles or saplings, about 10 feet high. Tie three poles together with nylon twine about one foot from the top of each pole. Set these three poles on the inner circle, forming a tripod, and anchor them into the ground. Lean the remaining poles up against the tripod and anchor them along the inner circle, forming a tipi-style structure. This is known as a *wickiup*.

5. In the area between the outer circle and the inner circle, create mounds of loose soil two feet in diameter and six to 12 inches high. Make the mounds two to three feet apart symmetrically around the circle.

6. At the center of each mound, plant eight corn seeds. These can be thinned to four corn plants after several weeks of growth.

5. In two weeks, sow two or three pole bean seeds six inches from each of the emerging corn plants and also around the base of each pole of the wickiup. Strings can be tied horizontally between the poles at one-foot intervals to trellis the pole beans.

6. Around the outer rim of each mound, sow several squash and/or pumpkin seeds (or seedlings). Eventually, the squash should be thinned to two to three per mound. Sister Bean fixes nitrogen and uses corn as a ladder. And Sister Squash, with her prickly vines, keeps out four-legged pests.

Extensions:

1. Save seeds every season to add to a local seed source. Create an area seed bank!

2. Invite Native American elders in your area to participate in laying out and planting the Three Sisters Garden.

The Nutrition Garden

The growing popularity of the USDA Food Guide Pyramid in schools is helping to change the eating habits of children everywhere. This increased nutritional awareness has inspired school-aged children to grow their own foods from the various food groups. Cultivating different vegetables that contain specific nutrients helps children apply the fundamental concepts of the Pyramid to their everyday lives. This is the foundation for building a lifelong appreciation and understanding of growing food and maintaining a healthy diet.

TOMATOES AND CARROTS

SWEET POTATOES

SQUASH AND PUMPKINS

Laid out in the shape of the letter "A," this Nutrition Garden contains crops with high amounts of vitamin A, aiding vision and digestion.

There are many ways to design and lay out a nutrition garden based on the Food Guide Pyramid's dietary principles. One method is to create a triangular garden in the shape of the Pyramid itself, with food crops that correspond to each of the food groups (see page 64).

The nutrition garden shown above is a Vitamin A Garden layed out in the shape of the letter "A." All the food crops grown in this garden contain high amounts of vitamin A, which aids vision and digestion. Gardens can also be designed in the shape of the letter "C" with vitamin C-filled crops, "D" for vitamin D crops, and so on.

The Vitamin A Nutrition Garden: Step-by-Step

1. Stake out a 20-by-20 foot area. Out of this square, stake out the shape of the letter "A," as shown in the drawing above.

2. Till the area and create four raised beds and narrow walkways between them. The width of the beds should be three to four feet, so that plants can be easily cared for from either side of the bed.

3. Plant seeds according to the planting scheme above, using spacing requirements from the seed packs.

4. Create signs to indicate the name of the vegetable, its vitamin content, and various ways to eat it. The signs are particularly instructive when they are made by the children themselves, integrating arts into the nutrition lesson. These signs can educate the wider community as well.

The Pizza Garden

I t doesn't take a certified dietitian to know that one of the favorite foods of almost any child in America is pizza. The Pizza Garden provides the perfect motivation for children to learn to grow their own food. The aim of the Pizza Garden is to enable children to grow as many of the ingredients as possible for making their own pizzas.

The Pizza Garden: Step-by-Step

Depending on the space available, pizza gardens can range in size from 10 to 50 feet in diameter.

1. Hammer a one-foot stake in the center of the garden. Attach string to the stake and measure to the outside edge of the garden space. (Kite string is cheap and easy to cut.) The length of the string—i.e., the distance from the center to the outside edge—is the radius of the circle. Typically, a 10-foot radius is sufficient. Tie the end of the string onto a hand-held stake.
2. Holding the stake and keeping the string taut, begin walking a circle on the outside edge of the garden. Drive a stake into the ground every two steps (or four to five feet). Continue around until you have reached your first stake and completed the circle.
3. Demarcate the circle perimeter by connecting the stakes with string.
4. Define the pizza slices by making walkways from one stake, through the center of the circle, to a stake on the opposite side.
5. Divide the pizza into eight beds (or slices) of equal size.
6. Carve out a small observational sitting area in the center of the circle.
7. Shovel the soil out of each walkway into the beds on either side.
8. Rake the beds so that they are level on top and slightly tapered at the edges. This maximizes growing space and minimizes erosion.

Important note: Each bed can be planted with its own individual crop, or every bed can be planted with a mixture of plants that complement one another. For example, onions, tomatoes, and basil make good companions and can be planted together in one bed. For the ambitious, wheat can be planted along the outer

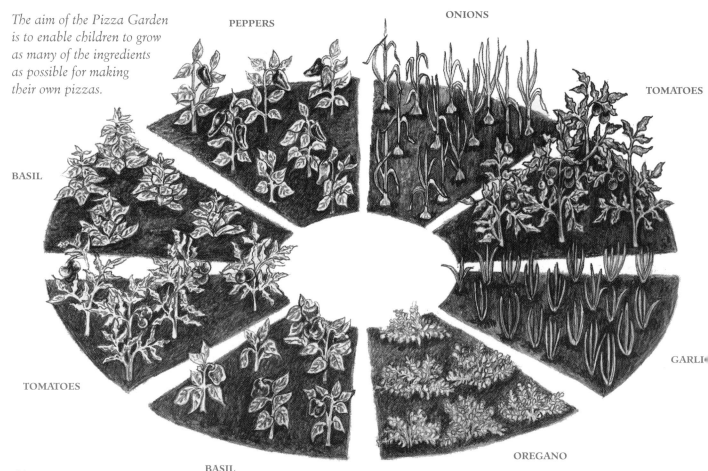

The aim of the Pizza Garden is to enable children to grow as many of the ingredients as possible for making their own pizzas.

PEPPERS

ONIONS

TOMATOES

BASIL

TOMATOES

GARLIC

BASIL

OREGANO

rim of the garden to make pizza crust. A good complement to a Pizza Garden is a Salsa Garden, which highlights herbs and spices.

The Community Mosaic Garden

The Community Mosaic Garden consists of an imaginative mix of theme gardens reflecting the many cultures, generations, and interests of a community. One of the major purposes of the Mosaic Garden is to provide expression for the diverse voices that echo through every neighborhood, village, and town. Ideally, the many different elements of the mosaic blend into an integrated whole, creating a unique harmony between the human and natural world.

Because every community is different, there is no formula for creating a community mosaic garden. The mosaic takes shape by merging into one working landscape the many theme gardens that grow from local needs and tastes.

The garden pictured on the next page has a number of features that may be adapted to fit any school or community garden.

Arbors. This simple woven-sapling entrance-way, with climbing morning glories, provides a magical opening to the pathways that circulate through the different theme gardens.

Pathways. Well-marked, clearly defined pathways naturally attract visitors to explore the wonders of the garden. The layout of the pathways can take many forms, from straight rows to flowing curves. They should, however, always maintain a minimum width of two to three feet in order to make the gardens accessible to elders, as well as wheelchairs and garden carts. The pathways can be lined with attractive materials that inhibit weed growth, such as bark mulch, wood chips, pea stone, straw, or sawdust.

The Center Courtyard. Whether placed directly at the geometric center of the garden or at a main intersection of the major pathways, the courtyard is a special area of the Mosaic Garden that allows people to interact with one another. Inspired by the village commons of New England, the courtyard provides a dynamic space to share the old-fashioned art of conversation. Combined with container gardens, the courtyard itself can also be a place for vegetable, herb,

and flower growing. The courtyard is an open invitation to share food, stories, music, poetry, and local entertainment in the garden, including student presentations and performances. During the summer months and on evenings and weekends, it can also be a classroom for community education including hands-on gardening and nutrition workshops, discussion groups, and creative arts classes.

Wild Botanical Garden. The art of agriculture involves altering the natural landscape according to human needs, too often with little regard for native species. The Wild Botanical Garden, usually located in a corner of the Community Mosaic Garden, is an "ecology island" that is allowed to grow wild. This is a sanctuary for native species, and provides beneficial habitat for birds and insects to maintain a balanced and interdependent garden ecosystem.

Trees, shrubs, wildflowers, and native grasses are allowed to flourish in this section of the garden. Birdhouses, feeders, and birdbaths also can insure that this will be a favorite nesting ground and visiting place for area birdlife. Interpretive displays and signs describing some of the flora will demonstrate that this is a welcome home for native species that provide the biological diversity essential for all life.

Multi-use Arts and Cooking Circle. Certainly one of the driving inspirations of youth gardening is the hands-on nutrition education that sustains a child's growth. Merely cultivating vegetables, herbs, and flowers is only one part of the gardening story. Growing one's own food also yields culinary gratification as gardeners prepare and eat the fruits of their labor. Having a space devoted strictly to the culinary arts insures that participants gain an in-depth appreciation, knowledge, and understanding of the whole nutrient cycle.

The Cooking Circle can include a fire pit at the center for preparing foods, surrounded by benches. A bulletin board on the outer ring provides a useful place for putting up notices, schedules, and posters focusing on weekly themes. The outdoor kitchen should be stocked with a number of cooking supplies including plates, silverware, cookware, spices, and food-storage containers. A Cooking Circle might also include a canning and drying area, a solar oven, an outdoor wood-fired bread oven, and a simple pantry for storing and preserving foods.

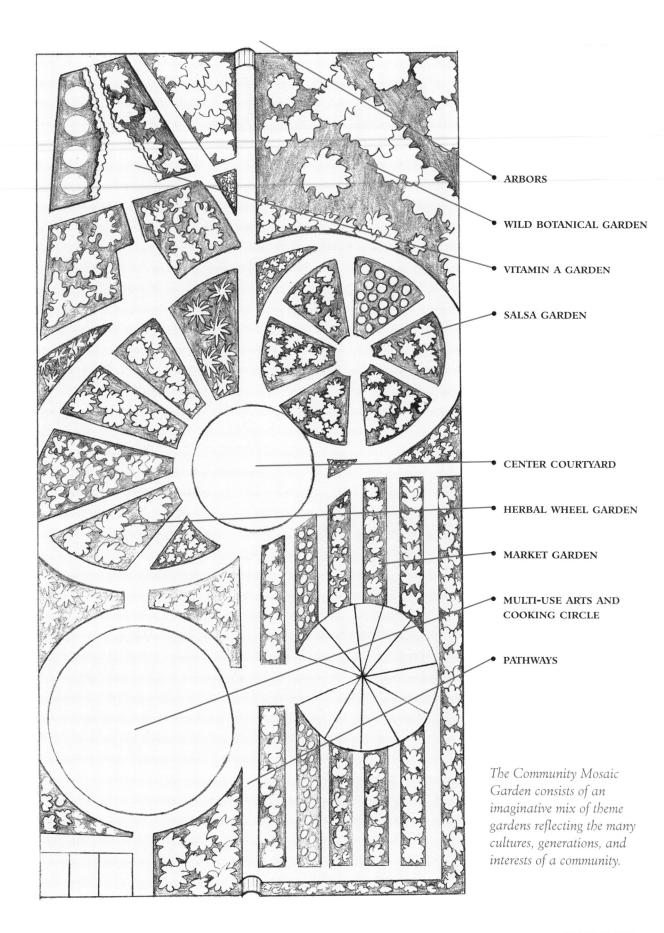

ARBORS

WILD BOTANICAL GARDEN

VITAMIN A GARDEN

SALSA GARDEN

CENTER COURTYARD

HERBAL WHEEL GARDEN

MARKET GARDEN

MULTI-USE ARTS AND COOKING CIRCLE

PATHWAYS

The Community Mosaic Garden consists of an imaginative mix of theme gardens reflecting the many cultures, generations, and interests of a community.

More Garden Design Ideas

Most of the following garden design ideas are for container gardens; however, any one of these plans can be constructed as a straight-row or raised-bed garden.

A Child's Garden (Kindergarten)

This garden is designed for younger children and includes easy-to-grow vegetables such as lettuce, spinach, and peas, plus simple flowers like marigolds and daisies. Be sure to make wide walkways and include small wooden benches for children to rest on, as well as a play area in the center for games and stories.

Butterfly Garden

This container is built in the shape of a butterfly with flowers and other features that attract these beautiful creatures for which the garden is named. Locate the garden in a very sunny area that will naturally attract butterflies, and include flat rocks and shallow puddles for butterflies to land on or near. Also, plant a variety of different flowers to offer a wide spectrum of color and to allow for a continuous bloom throughout the warm months. Some common plants that attract butterflies are cosmos, impatiens, zinnia, French marigolds, New England asters, dill, parsley, and azaleas.

Earth Garden

The Earth Garden contains raised beds in the shape of each of the seven continents. By growing foods indigenous to each continent in the corresponding container garden, children learn geography, agricultural history, economics, and development.

Sunflower House

This garden consists of sunflower plants grown in a circle wide enough for children to play in. Plant morning glories to grow up the outside of the house. Sunflower seeds can be baked and eaten, or they can be pressed to make sunflower oil. Another fun project is to make a sunflower maze.

Rainbow Garden

This flower garden boasts a wide variety of colorful annual and perennial flowers that can then be cut and sold. Start simple with bachelor buttons, statice, a wildflower mix, lupines, marigolds, dwarf sunflowers, asters, and junipers. Ask your local nursery for more ideas.

Market Garden

Row crops consisting mostly of vegetables, but also including herbs and flowers, are grown exclusively for sale at roadside stands, local farmer's markets, food stores, co-ops, and other retail outlets.

Market gardens are especially appealing to middle and high school kids who want to earn money from their hard labor. Profits from food sales can be set aside in a special bank account to be used later for special events, field trips, and garden improvements.

Be sure to space the planting of vegetables over several weeks in the springtime, so that all of the produce does not come to harvest at the same time.

Food Shelf Garden

This garden is a great way to contribute to the local food shelf. Children can coordinate the garden cultivation and recruit food shelf customers to help with weeding, mulching, watering, harvesting, and packaging. Besides exposing children to a wider spectrum of their community, a Food Shelf Garden helps to connect children to families in need in a meaningful way.

The Peacham School in northeast Vermont celebrates the origins of food from around the planet in their own Earth Garden.

Medicinal and Culinary Herb Garden

Grow local indigenous herbs for cooking and medicinal uses. Consult a local herbalist for tips on plants unique to your region that have healing properties. Contact an imaginative cook, chef, or homemaker who likes to grow his or her own spices. Ask for special tips on growing strategies for your climate and geography.

For a first-time Medicinal and Culinary Herb Garden, experiment with purple coneflower, yarrow, aloe, chamomile, angelica, comfrey, calendula, cilantro, basil, sage, oregano, and mint.

Call a nearby greenhouse for information on where to obtain the seeds (or starts) for these.

American History Garden

An American History Garden can be designed and constructed to depict the different geographic regions and agricultural patterns in the U.S. Built in the shape of the continental U.S., this garden can feature foods specific to the major regions of the country: wheat and corn in the Midwest; peanuts, cotton, and black-eyed peas in the Southeast; peppers, onions, and spices in the Southwest; potatoes and assorted roots crops in New England; and different greens and tomatoes in the Northwest.

Food Guide Pyramid Garden

Create a garden in the shape of the USDA Food Guide Pyramid. Plant it with foods corresponding to the various food groups. This provides a living, lively nutrition lesson throughout the growing season. (See activity, page 64.) Here are some suggestions of foods to grow in the raised beds of each food group:

- *Grains*: wheat, oats, barley, rye
- *Vegetables*: lettuce, spinach, carrots
- *Fruits*: strawberries, low-bush blueberries
- *Proteins*: soy beans, peanuts
- *Dairy*: substitute soy products to make soy milk or soy cheese; or bring in high-fat milk to make butter, cheese, yogurt
- *Fats, Sweets, Oils*: sunflowers for seeds and oil

Shakespeare Garden

The act of tilling the soil naturally inspires many forms of creative expression, especially the dramatic arts. Drawing from the inspiration of Shakespeare's work, many schools have created a natural amphitheater from their terraced container gardens. Gently sloping land makes a perfect site for a dramatic-arts space surrounded by container gardens that can also be used for seating.

You can plant flowers, herbs, and vegetables mentioned in Shakespeare's works, with markers including quotations.

TOP: *The Pomfret School in central Vermont used gently sloping land to create a Shakespeare Garden to give students an area to perform short plays on local history, their school, families, and their own lives.*

BOTTOM: *Designed by Cynthia Lafoe and her fifth grade students at Newport Town School in the Northeast Kingdom of Vermont, this American History Garden shows the geography of different regions of the U.S., and the various foods grown in those areas.*

Compost as a Microcosm of Community

– by Judy Elliot, Denver Urban Gardens Coordinator

Denver Urban Gardens (D.U.G.) is a nonprofit organization founded to sustain green spaces throughout the city. One of our projects is the Peace Garden, a large plot in a predominantly Hispanic neighborhood. The landscape consists of terraced growing areas, an orchard, and areas for soil improvement. It also includes an Aztec ballcourt, places for dances, graffiti art, and murals and memorial tiles for youths killed by gang violence.

Building the Peace Garden was hard but wonderful work. For many youngsters involved in the garden, creating and maintaining compost piles has provided a rare sense of order in their lives. The children soon grew to delight in tending their heaping piles of compost. They learned to use "trash" to create fertile soil. They came to appreciate the slow process of nurturing and caring for something, and taking pride in completing a task. In time, the compost pile became symbolic of this diverse community—each micro-organism playing a role in creating the "brown gold" for growing. For once, these children learned to appreciate diversity as an opportunity, instead of a threat.

At the peak of the season, the garden has bean and gourd tipis, circular ceremonial plantings of chilis, murals celebrating planting and harvesting, a small pond, and plaques highlighting Hispanic cultures. We have dried flowers both for selling as wreaths and for ceremonies like the Day of the Dead held in the Peace Garden.

With this single garden, we have brought together a barren piece of earth and barren lives; and in one year, both the earth and the lives it has touched have borne fruit. Creating healthy conditions for plants is not very different from creating a healthy environment for people. It is a slow, passionate process of caring and love.

Ana Chavez hauling weeds for compost making.

4

Bringing Designs to Life

TO TRY TO UNDERSTAND THE SOIL BY TAKING A FEW TROWELSFUL AND

SUBMITTING THEM TO CHEMICAL TESTS IS LIKE TRYING TO UNDERSTAND THE

HUMAN BODY BY [ANALYZING] A FINGER ... AND PERFORMING THE SAME

TESTS. YOU MAY LEARN A LOT ABOUT THE CHEMISTRY ...

BUT ABOUT THE INTRICATE ANATOMICAL LINKAGE OF SYSTEMS—AND ABOUT

THE BODY'S FUNCTIONS AS A WHOLE—YOU WILL LEARN NOTHING AT ALL.

– William Bryant Logan, *Dirt—The Ecstatic Skin of the Earth*

Carefully mapping out detailed program plans, activities schedules, and garden designs as outlined in the first three chapters is undoubtedly one key to organizing a successful, long-lived gardening program for children. Equally important, however, is transferring all of these best-laid plans from the drafting table to the garden bed in the great outdoors.

This chapter describes the do's and don'ts for locating an optimal space for a children's garden, mapping the site, creating a master design, tilling, laying out and building the garden beds, and developing simple planting strategies.

Locating the Garden Site

Where do you start? A good place to begin is the *Site Location Criteria Checklist* on page 32. These critical questions help determine whether a garden site is ideal or not.

Of course, there is no ironclad rule that every successful gardening project must unfold according to the organizational stages outlined here. Often, identifying the garden site is the *first* step that inspires the rest

of the process—committees forming, funds being raised, and programs developing. The aim here is to outline the essential bases that must be covered to make the operation workable and sustainable. Each group's unique circumstances will dictate the logical order in which the activities must be performed.

The garden site that is most readily available frequently determines the plans and aspirations for the design, rather than the other way around. If the most viable spot available to you is an abandoned lot that measures 30 by 50 feet, then that will shape the nature of the garden you grow. It is rare to find a plot that fits a long list of prespecified criteria. The art of planning is to be able to reconcile imagination with reality.

The site location and design process works best with the help of a group of volunteers. It would be unrealistic to expect one person to have the time and energy to complete all the tasks outlined in this chapter. Don't forget about the most important aspect to this process—community involvement. And don't forget to solicit advice and help from experienced growers. They are by far your most valuable local resource.

Site Location Criteria Checklist

Finding the ideal site for a children's garden may prove to be a challenging exercise. Use the following checklist as a guide in your search for a site suitable to your needs. Elements of a workable garden site include:

❏ **ACCESS:** Is this site conveniently located for those who will be using it most? Try to site the garden near the neighborhood of likely participants.

❏ **SOIL QUALITY:** Is the soil loose enough to hold seeds and compact enough to hold water? Dig a few one- to two-foot-deep test holes in different spots on the site to get a profile of soil consistency. Soil with clay, sand, rocks, or rubble may need special attention.

❏ **SOIL SAFETY:** Is the soil free of chemical pollution? (*Caution*: some sites are available for use *because* they are hazardous!) Ask neighbors if they know of the history of the site, particularly if any toxic chemicals were ever dumped there. If there is a possibility there has been dumping at the site, have the soil tested.

❏ **PERSONAL SAFETY:** Is the site safe from vandalism, dogs, foot traffic, etc?

❏ **SIZE:** Does the site have space for a large number of children, as well as tools, wheelbarrows, and a diversity of activities?

❏ **SUNLIGHT:** Does the site receive at least eight hours of sun per day?

❏ **WATER:** Is there access to water nearby?

❏ **AVAILABILITY:** Is the site available for garden use now, and can it remain available in future years?

Have the Organizing Committee list the strengths and weaknesses of the site, along with any other important considerations specific to that location.

Attunement: Getting to Know the Existing Natural Ecosystem

Before people change any natural area to fit their needs, it is crucial to make certain that the human agenda blends with the existing ecosystem. Whenever human beings alter the land, there are consequences to the natural inhabitants, the flora and fauna, and ultimately to people themselves.

In the exercise at left, the key questions participants ask are:

* Where in this "nature garden" can we see examples of basic ecological principles such as diversity, unity, interdependence, etc.?

* How can we design our garden naturally, keeping these same ecological principles in mind?

* If a sustainable garden ecosystem is here already, how do we find our niche in it?

With these questions in mind, we are ready to read the landscape.

Designing the Site

When a site has been found that meets the site location criteria, a master plan can be drawn up for a multi-use garden site. This design process will allow you to map the major natural and human-made features of the site and determine the size and location of each garden feature relative to the others. Complete step-by-step directions for all four stages of the design process summarized below can be found in Appendix B.

Creating a Base Map— Marking the Boundaries

A base map is a simple scale drawing marking the boundaries of the garden, and designating compass points. While children can be actively involved in this stage of the project, the garden organizers should take particular care that the boundary distances are measured and recorded, and the approximate angles are calculated reasonably accurately.

Site Analysis—Reading the Landscape

After the boundaries are recorded on the base map, the size and location of the natural and human-made elements on the site must be drawn. Are there trees, footpaths, or unusual amounts of litter on the land?

Five Levels of Attuning to the Garden Site

Purpose: To attune the group to the natural ecosystem at the garden site.

Discovery Question: What already lives in the habitat we have designated for the garden?

Materials: Field guides (birds, trees, wildflowers, animal tracks), pens and paper, hand lenses, binoculars, and string.

Procedure:

1. Look at the big picture.

- Find a place to sit that provides a good view of the entire site. Sit silently, and survey this new environment. Listen, smell, feel, breathe, and imagine yourself as part of this ecosystem. What do you see going on? Who lives here? What plants are growing here?
- What stages of ecological succession can be seen in this habitat: cleared meadow, bramble-thicket, young tree saplings, a full forest?
- Observe and sketch the big picture.

2. Identify a specific flower, shrub, or tree.

- Sit with the plant, observe and sketch. What does this species depend on for its survival? What depends on it to survive (insects, birds, other plants)?
- Record all observations using a notebook and pen or pencil. Sketch or list what you see, sense, feel, hear, taste, and smell.

3. Get a ground-level view.

- Get down on your hands and knees to observe what is happening on the ground: ants, spiders, caterpillars, animal signs, plants, rocks, etc.
- With a hand lenses, look for both flying and non-flying ground insects. Who lives at the soil level? Observe and sketch.
- What do they depend on for survival?
- What animal signs can you detect? Look for tracks or scat (droppings) of rabbits, squirrels, raccoons, skunks, and birds.

4. Go underground.

- Shovel up some soil to see what is underfoot. Observe soil colors and textures, earthworms and microorganisms that are recycling nutrients to feed the plants. Record.

5. How does this all fit together?

- Sort and classify as many components at each of these levels as possible—macro, individual, ground level, and below ground.
- Trace the indigenous natural food web. There is a garden growing here already. What insects, plants, birds, and wildlife are feeding on the foods produced by the flowers, seeds, and fruits living here?
- Which species depend on which other species for their survival?
- Consider ways to integrate your plans for annual and perennial food production into the existing natural food web.

Extension:

- Invite a forester, cooperative extension agent, field biologist, or high school biology teacher to visit the site to help explain the biological highlights of this habitat. You can learn about the whole world from this site.

Are there signs of animal habitats? The first step is to look and observe; then record on the base map; and finally evaluate the potential usefulness and impact of these elements on the garden program.

Preliminary Site Design—
Brainstorming the Possibilities

Now comes the fun part: What garden design ideas will fit the dimensions and physical characteristics of this site? Be wild and creative—and flexible. Design ideas are written in pencil on tracing paper placed over the base map, so that adjustments can be made quickly and easily.

Master Plan—
Creating a Final Garden Design

In this last stage of the process, a master garden blueprint is determined based on the designs created above. The exact size and location of each garden theme area is sketched onto the base map. (For more detailed planting strategies within each garden area, see Chapter Three.)

Tilling, Laying Out, and Building the Garden

This section details everything you need to know about laying out a garden site. The process is divided into three easy steps—clearing and tilling the site, staking and laying out the garden, and making beds and walkways.

The first year of work on a garden is always the most labor intensive. After the initial season, the soil can generally be worked using only hand tools. In each successive year, less labor is needed as the soil becomes easier to work. As beneficial habitat is restored, birds and insects return, and humans find their niche in this thriving environment.

Clearing and Tilling the Site

After the design process is complete, but before the garden can be tilled and planted, the site must be thoroughly cleared of all shrubs, brambles, trees, and other debris. Before clearing, be sure to identify and mark any perennials worth saving, such as flowers, berry bushes, or fruit trees. Mark them by tying orange surveyor's tape to their branches or stems. The courtyard areas can remain unplowed and seeded as a lawn. Clearing the site makes for a good volunteer clean-up day. Get the word out, and bring along some healthy snacks. You'll be amazed at how fast and efficient your crew will have the land cleared.

Now the soil can be tilled in preparation for planting. Depending on the size of the garden plot and the soil conditions, you may want to use a tractor with a power tiller, or ask a local farmer to plow and disc the site. The best time to till a garden is in the fall, so that you can plant a cover crop like buckwheat or winter rye. When spring emerges, or when the cover crop has become established, till it under to enrich the soil and reduce the spread of perennial grasses. Speak to a local farmer or agricultural extension agent about the best cover crop for your climate and soil.

Many gardeners work composted manures or composted kitchen wastes into the soil. Raw manures are harmful to soil microorganisms should never be used until they have had time to mellow for several months. See page 38 for more information on composting.

Often the plot needs to be cleaned and raked a second time after the soil is broken up. Pull out clumps of sod, rake out and gather piles of rocks, and break up the chunks of clay. (See *Weed Did It* in Chapter Five.) The rocks can be used to line walkways, drainage ditches, and talking circles and to decorate the smaller children's gardens.

As you work the soil, you will become more familiar with its quality and depth. The soil may be heavy clay or sandy loam. It may change from one end of the garden to the other. A good practice in a new garden is to conduct a soil test. Call your agricultural extension agent for details. Results of the test will help you determine what amendments are practical for growing certain crops. No matter what your soil type, all gardens will benefit from the addition of organic material. This includes leaf and grass composts, as well as composted kitchen scraps and stable manures.

Staking and Laying Out the Garden

You can now demarcate the garden beds, walkways, and other multi-use areas on the site. For this exercise, you will need several dozen wooden stakes, each 12 to 18 inches long and one-quarter to one-half inch thick. You will also need a ball of kite string, a knife, a hammer, and a tape measure. To lay out the garden, follow these easy steps:

1. Hammer a stake in the ground at each of the corners, leaving six to 12 inches remaining above the ground.

Garden beds are staked out and marked by string.

2. Run kite string along the outside borders of the garden, tying it to each of the corner stakes. This gives clear definition to the boundaries.
3. Determine the entrance of the primary walkway along one end of the site boundaries and mark it with a stake. Now determine the width of the walkway (a 42-inch-wide walkway will make the garden wheelchair accessible). Mark the width of the walkway entrance with another stake.
4. Cut the kite string in the middle of the walkway entrance. Tie each end of the string to each of the two stakes at the entrance. You now have an entrance to the garden.
5. Repeat these steps to mark the walkway at the opposite end of the garden.
6. Define the central walkway by tying a string from each stake at one end to the opposite stake at the other end of the garden.
7. If you would like more winding walkways to create a circulation loop, more stakes will be needed to demarcate smaller sections of the walkway boundaries. A garden hose is useful for shaping the curving edges of boundaries. Lay the hose down following one boundary edge of the wind-

ing walkway. Drive stakes along the edge of the hose at three- to four-foot intervals. To establish the other edge of the curved walkway, drive stakes directly across from the stakes along the curved garden hose.

This is the basic procedure for staking all garden areas. Variations of these steps can be repeated to stake out each area across the entire site.

Important note: Most people—especially children—tend not to walk in straight lines. Consider making some walkways curved rather than linear. This may take more time, but it will give the garden a freer form.

When the garden is staked out, step back and look at the design from a distance to determine:

1. Are the walkways wide enough, and do they connect all of the garden areas?
2. Is there enough room for young people and adults to mingle easily within each theme garden, multi-use area, courtyard, and central meeting area?
3. Do the raised beds and different theme gardens fit the unique needs of the children? For example, five- to seven-year-olds work better with smaller garden beds than 10- to 12-year-olds, whose arms are longer.

Once the garden is entirely staked out, it is not unusual to discover that the design is too complicated and there is not enough room for easy movement and circulation. Young children, for example, need more space to move than older children and adults. Take the opportunity to reevaluate the overall site design. Don't be afraid to tinker a little with the original plan—gardens, after all, are not set in stone.

Making Beds and Walkways

The following procedure describes how to make a raised-bed garden while digging walkways. If you are planning to build a container garden, refer to page 37.

1. Shovel topsoil from the walkways onto the garden bed areas to create a permanent path through the garden and to build up raised beds for cultivation. Shovel out paths four to eight inches deep. Use a wheelbarrow if necessary.
2. Rake out all walkways so that they are level.
3. Fill the walkways with bark mulch, pea stone, wood chips, old straw (stay away from hay, it has seeds), sand, landscape fabric, and even old carpet to inhibit weed growth, enhance appearance,

and aid drainage. Use whatever medium is readily available to clearly mark circulation paths through the garden. Often, local power companies, parks and rec departments, or city maintenance crews will have chipped mulch or bark mulch to donate.

4. If the soil in the beds has clumps of clay and is heavily compacted, it needs to be broken up with a spading fork before raking. Rake the beds out evenly, so that all the soil is of uniform depth. Make the soil level with a slight grade on the edge. Once the garden is constructed, all participants must know clearly they are not to walk on the garden beds.

Planting Strategies: The Basics

Once the beds and walkways have been constructed, encourage the children to use their botanical, mathematical, and artistic skills to determine planting patterns for each bed. If you have experienced gardeners working with you, plant varieties, spacing, and layout can be determined and mapped.

The cardinal rule for deciding what to plant in a youth garden is to choose vegetables that the children want to eat! This does not preclude experimenting with new foods, but as a rule of thumb, stick to what children say they want. Gradually introduce new or less popular foods one or two at a time.

When determining what to plant in the garden and where to plant it, the shape, width, and height of the plant at maturity should be known beforehand. Otherwise, you could overplant and get a smaller harvest, or underplant and waste valuable soil and space. Use the information on the back of the seed packets for the best planting strategies. For more complete descriptions of germination rates, spacing, mature plant size, etc., see *Rodale's Successful Organic Gardening* (Rodale Press, (610) 967-5171).

Following are three kinds of planting strategies you can use for your garden beds.

Single-Crop Beds

Plant one crop per bed. Space seedlings according to their size at maturity. For example, if you are planting lettuce, which matures to four inches, they should be planted eight inches from each other.

Single-crop beds are especially good for succession planting—seeds of the same crop are planted every couple of weeks, yielding a continual harvest over the course of the season.

Mixed Beds

Grow a number of different crops in each bed. For salad making, grow a diversity of plants in separate rows in the beds. Consider multi-story planting, such as growing a tall crop, like broccoli, beside lettuce.

Geometric Design

Incorporate multiple shapes of plants to cover every inch of the bed. With this sophisticated version of a mixed bed, interplanting is more intense. The most complex and advanced geometric designs should be reserved for older children with previous garden experience who are ready for a new challenge.

In addition to using garden space in the most efficient manner, geometric beds are also self-mulching—mature plant leaves create a canopy to maintain moisture and soil quality.

Companion Planting

The art of companion planting involves growing a diversity of vegetables, flowers, and herbs in close proximity to one another in patterns that benefit all of the plants. Most herbs, for example, are good companions to vegetable crops because they tend to repel harmful pests that feed on many varieties of vegetables. Flowering plants tend to attract beneficial insects, including beetles and dragonflies, which in turn feed off plant-eating pests. In addition, you can maximize garden space by planting shallow-rooted crops like lettuce and spinach next to vegetables that have deep roots, like carrots, beats, and potatoes.

There is a wealth of material written on the subject of companion planting. Check your local library or bookstore for an in-depth look at this fascinating aspect of gardening.

Raised-Bed Gardening

Raised beds maximize food production by allowing plants to grow intensively on a three- to four-foot-wide area. To create a raised-bed garden, soil is shoveled from walkways and other non-growing areas onto the growing area, creating elevated garden beds. When shaping the beds, form a level surface on top so water will stay on the bed and not run off into the pathway. To protect the soil from compacting, participants should never step on the garden bed.

Benefits of Raised-Bed Gardens:

✔ greater food production
✔ less compacting of the soil
✔ more top soil in the growing area, aiding root development
✔ plants grow together in clusters, shading out weeds and preserving ground moisture
✔ efficient use of compost

The Raised Bed.

Container Gardening

With all the energy, sweat, and labor a garden requires, it is often most practical to construct container gardens made from untreated wood. Six-by-six-inch hemlock timbers laid on top of one another and spiked together will last for many years. These wood containers can be fashioned into any shape, including rectangles, squares, triangles, the shape of your state, the continents, the earth, or a butterfly.

Use only natural, untreated woods to build a container garden. Wood treated with polyurethane or other preservatives, including pressure-treated wood, contains harmful chemicals that will leach out and poison the soil.

The remaining garden designs in this chapter can be constructed as container gardens. This type of garden provides a practical method of growing plants with children for a number of reasons.

Benefits of Container Gardens:

✔ keeps creeping weeds out
✔ gardening area stays neat and organized
✔ easy to care for
✔ minimal work required after construction
✔ attractive appearance will last for many years
✔ intergenerational and wheelchair accessible
✔ loose and well-drained soil optimizes nutrient availability
✔ can be shaped to fit any design
✔ prevents trampling and compacting of the soil
✔ allows easy access to all areas of the garden bed, permitting intensive, efficient planting
✔ offers a place to sit, relax, and become inspired by growing life

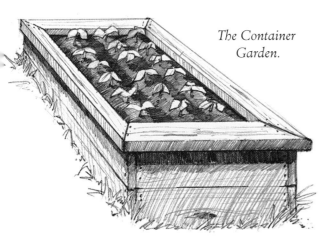

The Container Garden.

Behold this compost! behold it well!

Perhaps every mite has once formed part of a sick person—yet behold!

The grass of spring covers the prairies ...

The resurrection of the wheat appears with pale visage out of its graves ...

Out of its little hill faithfully rise the potato's dark green leaves,

Out of its hill rises the yellow maize-stalk, the lilacs bloom in the dooryards,

The summer growth is innocent and disdainful above all those strata of sour dead.

– Walt Whitman, *This Compost*

Composting

No garden would be complete without a compost pile. Compost, from the Latin *compositus*, is a mixture of organic waste—including food scraps, leaves, and grass—combined with soil and manure that is used for fertilizing and conditioning the soil. When the organic matter is broken down by microorganisms and other decomposers, it becomes rich, fertile humus, perfect for growing strong and healthy plants.

Compost is a crucial element of the garden ecosystem. Having a well-cared-for compost system completes the food cycle on the garden site—from seed to soil, to plants to food, to waste to compost, and back to soil again. On-site compost is the most efficient means of feeding the garden because it takes the "waste" produced by the garden and returns it back to the soil as food for plants. Good compost helps create soil with better aeration, better water retention, and more resistance to erosion. Compost repays the soil for what the garden has taken out in vegetables, fruits, and flowers. Compost is the legal tender of nature, the currency of life itself, because it continually pays back the nutrients the soil needs to continually regenerate itself.

Testing the Soil

Soil tests can range from the very complex (laboratory testing for a wide range of soil nutrients) to the very simple (on-site testing for pH). In either case, small amounts of soil should be taken from

Testing the soil.

various parts of the garden, then mixed together to obtain an accurate profile of overall soil conditions.

To test for important soil nutrients essential for healthy plant growth, such as nitrogen, phosphorous, potassium, calcium, and magnesium, contact a local agricultural extension agency though a nearby college or university. They will either mail out all the materials for collecting samples, or send an agent to your garden site to collect soil samples and discuss the soil characteristics with you.

Testing the pH of the soil—the soil's acidity—is an interesting learning activity that involves placing a soil sample in an extractive solution and determining the pH of the solution on special alkaline/acid test paper. For kits on testing pH and NPK (nitrogen, phosphorous, potassium) and conducting other soil experiments, call Let's Get Growing, (800) 408-1868.

Building a Three-Bin Composter

Materials: 10 wooden pallets of equal size, approximately 40 inches square; 14 cedar posts, six feet in length and two inches in diameter; six cedar posts, four feet in length and two inches in diameter; one roll of chicken wire or hardware cloth, 50 feet in length and three feet wide; 10 to 20 feet of 14 gauge wire; one pound fence staples.

Procedure:

1. Stand one of the wooden pallets straight up so that the pallet strips run parallel to the ground. Place two six-foot cedar posts through the space between the pallet strips and pound them into the ground with a sledge hammer, supporting the pallet at each end. If the ground is hard, use an iron bar to start a pilot hole for the posts.

2. Continue setting up pallets to form the back wall and three side walls as shown in the drawing below. After you have set up seven pallets, you will have a three-bin composting system.

3. To strenghten the walls, wire together the cedar posts wherever the pallets are joined at a right angle.

4. Cover the inside of all three bins with chicken wire or hardware cloth using fence staples. Also, staple chicken wire to one side of each of the three pallets, which will act as doors to the finished structure.

5. Use the remaining three pallets as doors. Secure each one tightly against the side walls with wire when adding compost materials to the bins.

Roofing your compost bins:

A compost pile works best when moist. Insufficient moisture reduces compost digestion, while too much water causes it to be anaerobic (lacking air) and smelly. Roofing a compost bin will help create the perfect environment. Make the roof sloping downward from front to back, so that rainwater will drip down behind the pile and people will have an easier time adding to and shoveling the pile.

Materials: two 12-foot 2x6 beams; six four-foot 2x4 joists; five 12-foot 1x3 wooden straps; roofing material of choice (sheetmetal, plywood, tarp); one pound each of 12d common galvanized nails, 8d common galvanized nails, and galvanized roofing nails.

1. Make sure the front posts are at least a foot taller than the rear posts.

2. Nail a 12-foot 2x6 beam across the top of the front posts, and another across the top of the back posts, with 12d nails.

3. Nail the four-foot 2x4 rafters into the top of the beams every two feet with 12d nails.

4. Nail the 1x3 strapping to the rafters, 12 inches apart, with 8d nails.

5. Attach roofing material to the strapping: tarp, sheetmetal, or plywood.

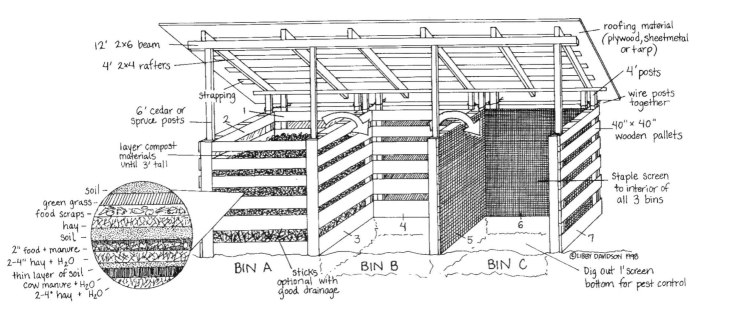

12' 2x6 beam
4' 2x4 rafters
strapping
6' cedar or spruce posts
layer compost materials until 3' tall
soil
green grass
food scraps
hay
soil
2" food + manure
2-4" hay + H₂O
thin layer of soil
cow manure + H₂O
2-4" hay + H₂O
BIN A
sticks optional with good drainage
BIN B
BIN C
roofing material (plywood, sheetmetal or tarp)
4' posts
wire posts together
40" x 40" wooden pallets
staple screen to interior of all 3 bins
©LIBBY DAVIDSON 1998
Dig out 1' screen bottom for pest control

Listening with Respect: Issues of Class and Race in Working the Land

– by Karen Payne, Program Director, American Community Gardening Association

When they hear that I'm involved with community gardening and children's gardening, people often say, "Oh, isn't it the greatest thing for kids. Don't the children just love being in the garden?" In my experience—and from what I hear when listening to teachers and parents—some kids love the garden and others can't stand it. Just like the adults I know. Some of my best friends don't like gardening. They love fresh food, they love flowers, most of them like looking at beautiful gardens, but they have absolutely no interest in growing any of it.

In working with From the Roots Up, a mentorship program that helps new community garden organizations, I hear quite a lot about challenges as well as successes in starting gardens. In addition to the individual responses people have to the opportunity to cultivate a patch of earth, I have come to see that there are significant social and cultural meanings attached to gardening and agriculture, which have an impact on people's responses to working the soil. Not surprisingly, these meanings apply to children as well. The differences can be related to a child's race, culture, or class—as well as their individual personalities and experiences.

Age can also make a difference. Many pre-school and elementary school children of all cultural backgrounds seem to experience the garden as fun, a time to explore the wonders of nature and play in the dirt. By the time they get to middle school, however, clothes, status, and the intense pressures of conformity tend to be much more important. Working or playing with dirt is not particularly good for any of those things. Thus issues concerning race and class tend to arise much more among middle or high school students (and their teachers and parents) than among younger children.

Our culture values technology, speed, and convenience. Growing food on a small scale highlights none of those things. All of us have been exposed to the ideals of progress; we are led to believe that large scale is more efficient than small scale and that technologi-cal advances are supposed to eliminate manual labor. In addition, stereotypes about working the land are not usually positive.

We can't expect children (or their parents and teachers) to suddenly transcend the values and the judgments of the society they live in. It is not so surprising when today's students feel that garden work is stupid. They reflect mainstream American values in their conviction that working the land is

> low **S**tatus,
> low **T**ech,
>   **U**ndervalued knowledge
> low **P**ay,
>   **I**rrelevant and inconsequential
> and **D**irty.

Plus it messes up fashionable sneakers.

Sometimes, it is the parents or teachers who are upset that their children are gardening as part of their school work. Isn't this just exactly the kind of back-breaking toil they hoped their kids would escape by getting an education? How dare the teachers make them take time away from "learning"?*

Parents and teachers seem to be pleased that their children are learning gardening when they perceive that it is reviving a valuable tradition that is in danger of being lost, probably because they or their people have had some good experiences of growing food. But some parents, teachers, and children see only oppression and exploitation in agricultural work, because that is what they or their people have experienced. As a white woman who has always had the option of not growing food, I feel that I need to listen deeply in order to understand the diverse meanings gardening has for people.

---

*It is worth noting that research has shown that children involved in school gardening projects actually learn better in all subject areas, not just those associated with the garden.

Given the legacy of slavery, sharecropping, and farm labor in this country, one of my African-American friends was appalled when she heard that African-American children were being forced to work in gardens even when they didn't want to (in some places, it is required as part of their school curriculum). One day, I saw just how real this history is for the children when an African-American boy who hated being in the garden was instructed by a white teacher to pull weeds. Even though I know that teachers are always in the position of telling children to do things they don't want to do, I felt uncomfortable seeing a black person being told by a white person to work the soil. Just then, two girls walked by and taunted, "Slave!"

And yet. There are countless examples of African-American youth (and children of every ethnic background) who started off hating dirt, but after a time, became proud of every vegetable they grew and ardent in their care of the garden. One solution to the problem of their initial distaste for working the land would be to avoid those situations in which we are reminded of the painful legacy of slavery or other forms of exploitation. But another strategy is to face it.

Shyaam Shabaka, founder of the Strong Roots gardening program, which works primarily with African-American youth, talks about "restoring African Americans to the lost agricultural heritage which is rightfully theirs." This heritage has to do with learning about nutritional, traditional African-American food crops, such as sweet potatoes, peanuts, and many types of greens. It is about honoring and connecting with ancestors and elders who offer a positive perspective on the values and traditions of African-American culture, as well as agricultural knowledge. It is about the right to own land and the hope for economic power and self-sufficiency. Asian Americans, European Americans, and Latino Americans can also take pride and pleasure in their people's agricultural wisdom and skills, despite the history of exploitation and poverty that is so often the reality of people who work the land.

A sense of connection to the earth is every human's birthright. The fact that oppression has caused many people to feel disconnected from growing food is a tragedy. Gardening is a pleasure for some people, but for others it is a reminder of a traumatic past.

We know quite a lot about how to value cultural differences and how to heal traumatic wounds. Although the garden has many negative associations, both with past evils and with current values, it also has the potential to heal some of those wounds. But for the garden to be healing, it takes more than the nurturing power of soil and sun and growing things.

The garden can be a place where self-respect grows, and students who may not do well in the classroom can have a new chance in a different context. The garden can be a haven where no one is ever shamed. Everyone can slow down. We can learn to listen with respect to children's ideas, validate their feelings, and tell the truth about the history of our peoples....There are many paths to healing and, always, you gotta have heart.

YOU GOTTA HAVE HEART

History is a key. Almost every race and culture has a history in which knowing how to work with the earth to grow food was considered an act of intelligence and an important spiritual activity, as well as a matter of survival. Our mission as garden educators is to help children recover that age-old wisdom for themselves.

Earth knowledge is valuable. In this age of technology and speed, it is important to offer students compelling reasons to value traditional practices such as gardening and cooking.

Art and Creativity are for everyone. It is necessary to give students a significant role in creative discussions and decision-making. Gardening is an art as well as a science. If "experts" design the garden, decide what to plant, and when and where, etc., the students are much more likely to see their role as unpaid labor, rather than feeling a sense of pride and ownership as gardeners.

Respect each person's story. Listen with respect to the reasons children give for liking and disliking garden work. Look for and validate the connections with their people's histories.

Testify to the value of cultural identity and the wrongness of oppression. Take an active role in helping people think about how issues of race and culture impact students' experiences in the garden. Always look for ways to be an ally to others who are raising these issues, and for allies to support you when you do this work.

5

Breaking Ground: Activities for Spring

At last, spring has arrived! It's planting time. This chapter contains five hands-on activities for school-age children to get some dirt under their nails and experience under their belts. The next 10 pages encompass what you need to know about starting seedlings indoors, planting outdoors with children, weeding without tears, and documenting the plants that are growing in the garden during the early weeks of the season. Additionally, Appendix A, Horticultural Basics, contains necessary information for successful seed starting.

First Days in the Garden

During the first few days in the garden, children usually benefit from a number of simple team-building exercises combined with stories, hands-on planting activities, and food-related nutrition exercises.

On the very first day, it is important to go over the many benefits of local food gardening, explaining why the kids truly are pioneers by participating in sustainable, organic food growing at the community level. Ask the children:

- ✔ Where does the food we buy at the store come from? Who grows it? How does it get here?
- ✔ Do you think it is important to grow your own food? Why?
- ✔ How do we grow our own food? What would we need to do to grow food here? How do we start?
- ✔ What food can be grown here?
- ✔ What would this place look like if we had food growing everywhere?

As children respond to these questions, the facilitator should repeat the thoughts and feelings expressed to the group as a whole, so that everyone can learn from each other.

The following activities are designed to get the children started on gardening. Some are single-day activities; others, like Indoor Magic, can be done over a period of days or weeks.

Opening Ceremony

To kick off your gardening program, host a Garden Opening Ceremony. When the soil has been turned over, the walkways built, the garden beds made, and the danger of frost has past, it is time to plant. Let the planting begin with a gala Opening Ceremony that involves the entire community.

The following page offers key elements for organizing such an event. Of course, opening ceremonies can be held at any time during the year, not only in spring. In any case, take the opportunity at the ceremony to organize volunteers into work teams to perform timely garden chores.

Opening Ceremony at the Earth Garden in Peacham, Vermont.

Holding an Exciting Kickoff Event

✔ *Plan well in advance.* If you are scheduling a ceremony for early June, begin planning in April.

✔ *Schedule the event for the right day of the week.* Saturday morning is a good time. This tends to be slow for the local paper looking for a feature event for the Sunday edition. Don't take up the whole day. A solid morning of well-prepared activities will bring good results.

✔ *Plan fun activities for children, especially preschoolers.*

✔ *Include food.* At the very least, you want to provide coffee and tea, juice or cider, and some wholesome snacks. Invite a local restaurant to donate food (and give them sponsorship billing).

✔ *Invite everyone.* Send special invitations to your school board, local movers and shakers, and politicos.

✔ *Involve local "celebrities."* They can share stories, songs, or legends for which they are famous around town.

✔ *Invite no more than three people to speak.* Limit their remarks to two or three minutes each. Focus for the day should be on the garden.

✔ *Display attractive, easy-to-read information.* This can be educational materials on various topics: community events, local issues, safe food, nutrition, and food co-ops. If you have a newsletter, give it out to those in attendance or sell it as a fundraiser.

✔ *Have sign-up sheets on hand.* These allow people to volunteer for projects on the spot. List the different jobs that need to be done, and ask each person to specify the type of work he or she is interested in. Also, list items needed. This will encourage donations.

✔ *Alert the local media early and often.* Send out public service announcements early. Many newspapers require one to three weeks of lead time to post local events in their community calendar. Contact editors about doing an advance story on the event and remind them of the great photo opportunities for the Sunday paper. Contact local TV and/or radio about doing a live broadcast of the ceremony.

✔ *Prepare a clear schedule of events.*

A typical schedule of events for a community youth garden Opening Ceremony might look something like this:

9:00 *Welcome.* Acknowledgments and introductions by the project organizer. Congratulatory message and expression of support by the mayor or local dignitary.

9:15 *Children's presentation.* Involve the hopes and plans of the community for the garden and unveil a sign, mural, or art project. Have children recite poems and sing songs.

9:30 *Ceremonial first seed planting.* This can be done by an elder or clergy member. Seeds are distributed while program leaders demonstrate planting methods. (See *Indoor Magic*, next page).

10:00 *Team work.* Have young adults prepare beds, make fences, build compost bins, or lead any timely activity. Be prepared with tools, plans, and leaders to coordinate projects.

Games and activities for children.

10:45 *Meal or snack.*

11:30 *Thanks.* Give a reminder of upcoming garden activities.

Indoor Magic
Starting Seedlings Indoors

Purpose: To begin growing plants from seeds for transplanting later in the garden; to document the progress of seedling growth.

Discovery Question: How and when do we start seeds growing indoors in order to have transplants ready at the start of the growing season?

Working Tools: Plant trays (flats), cell packs (inserts for the flats), potting soil (organic preferred), wooden or plastic labels (craft sticks work well), markers, clear plastic wrap (like Saran Wrap) to cover the flats, watering can, grow lights if available, and seeds.

Learning Tools: Paper, pencil, notebooks, colored pencils, crayons, seed catalogues for reference, and general plant reference texts.

Procedure:

1. Make sure all flats and cell packs are clean.
2. Premoisten the potting soil to the wetness of a wrung-out sponge.
3. Fill the cell packs to the top with the potting soil. Tap the packs on the floor to settle the soil down.
4. Hand out seeds to children. Place seeds in the hand they don't write with.
5. Using the hand they write with, children should place one seed in each cell.
6. Place one more seed in each cell.
7. Place seeds on top of the soil. Once seeds are laid on top of the soil, sprinkle soil over the top. Gently tap down soil with index finger.
8. Label each cell pack with the name of the plant and the date planted.
9. Line up the cell packs in the flats, and cover with clear plastic wrap. This will keep in moisture until germination occurs.
10. Place flats in a warm place until seeds begin to germinate.
11. After germination, remove the wrap, and place the flats under grow lights, or in a sunny, south-facing window. Important: If using grow lights, be sure the lights are only two to three inches above the plants.

Important note: Some seeds are "afraid of the dark" and will not sprout without daylight. Don't cover these seeds with soil. Also, bigger seeds must be planted somewhat deeper. Read seed packets carefully.

12. Once the seeds have sprouted, make sure they don't dry out. Water often. The best way to water new seedlings is to pour water into the flat, so that the baby plants are not disturbed. Pour water an inch deep into the flats. Keep soil the consistency of a wet, wrung-out sponge. After a half hour, pour out any remaining water in the bottom of the flats.
13. As the plants grow, raise grow lights and keep them no more than three inches above the plant.
14. After the first leaves appear, you may have to thin or transplant some of the plants.
15. As the time nears to plant outdoors, the growing seedlings need to be "hardened off" to get them used to outdoor conditions. Place the flats outside in a shady, protected spot for a few hours each day, increasing gradually the amount of sunlight they receive and the total time outside. Be sure not to put young plants outside if the temperature is below 45 degrees.

Weed Did It!

Pulling and Identifying Weeds

What Is a Weed?

Even after careful tilling, different weeds and perennial grasses will still take root, trying to reestablish a perennial grassland. No matter what you do, you will be dealing with numerous perennial plants and grasses for the first few years. Many of these plants, however, do provide beneficial habitat for insects, and many are edible.

Encourage the children to identify the different plants that grow in and around your garden to determine which ones you want to keep and which ones to eradicate. At the same time, remind children to be considerate of other organisms in the garden. Who lives here? What is their role and responsibility in the ecology of the wider area? Observe what sprouts and grows in your garden bed. In your haste to weed out undesirable plants, you may be taking away a creature's home, or pulling out a desirable nitrogen-fixing plant, like clover. Everyone should consider the larger web of nature in the garden that weaves in and around our plots. Understand how human beings fit into the natural ecosystems of the area where you want to grow specific plants. Work with what is already there on the site.

The danger of overweeding is one of the reasons for adopting an ecological gardening approach, free of chemical pesticides, herbicides, fungicides, and fertilizers—which in the long run can do more harm than good.

Purpose: To clear all weeds out of the garden beds in preparation for planting, to identify the weeds in your garden beds, and to document findings in a weed book.

Discovery Questions: How do we clear the garden beds of all plant life that could compete with our garden plants? What are the weeds we pulled, and how can we catalogue them?

Working Tools: Hoes, three-pronged cultivators, buckets for collecting weeds.

Learning Tools: Large tray for weed specimens, corrugated cardboard (at least 12 inches by 12 inches), newspaper, bungee cords or heavy string, hand lenses, paper, pencil, notebooks, colored pencils, crayons, and field guides to weed types.

Common Weeds of the United States
Dover Publications
180 Varick Street, New York, NY 10014

Weeds, by Alexander Martin
Golden Guide Series, Western Publishing Co.
Dept. M, 1220 Mound Ave., Racine, WI 53404

WEED THE BEDS

1. After the soil is broken up, use hoes, cultivators, and hands to pull up all of the existing plant life remaining on the beds. Remove the entire plant and root to inhibit regeneration.
2. Reserve specimens of each plant in a separate tray.
3. Empty the rest into the compost pile.
4. Remove sticks, roots, trash, and anything else that is not soil.

Important note: If seed heads are clearly evident on the weed, do not put them in the compost pile, or they will reproduce in your compost. Throw away weeds that have gone to seed in a separate pile.

Extensions:

Weed-pulling Competition. Who can pull up the most weeds in five minutes? Who can find the longest root? Who can find the most varieties of weeds in five minutes? Which has the biggest leaves? The smallest leaves?

CREATE A PLANT PRESS

1. Take the weed specimens that were set aside in the tray in the previous exercise, *Weed Did It!*
2. Place newspaper over a 12 inches by 12 inches piece of corrugated cardboard. Place weed specimens of approximately the same thickness on the newspaper, making sure that they do not touch one another.
3. Place two sheets of newspaper on top of those specimens. The newspaper absorbs the moisture from the plants to dry them.
4. Place more weed specimens on top of the next layer of newspaper.
5. Cover those specimens with two more pieces of newspaper.
6. Continue this procedure as many times as there are weed specimens.
7. Cover the last layer with a layer of newspaper.
8. Place another 12 inches by 12 inches piece of cardboard on top.
9. Secure with bungee cords or heavy string.
10. Place a heavy stack of books or magazines on top of the whole thing.
11. Let sit for three to four days.
12. After three to four days, disassemble and check specimens for dryness. (If they are not dry, relayer and allow to sit for another three days.)
13. Once dry, glue the dried leaves in a Weed Book.

Extensions:

Improve Your Weed Book. Identify the weed specimens using a weed identification manual. Include the common and Latin names of each species.

How did this weed get here? Where did it originate? Is it edible? Does it provide a beneficial habitat for insects that are good for the garden? Why don't we want weeds in our garden? How can weeds be safely controlled? Research historical use of weeds: medicinal, culinary, decorative, etc.

Throughout the growing season, observe what weeds appear and where. Are they different than those originally found in the spring? Are there more or fewer? What new weeds appear? Press the new specimens and enter in your Weed Book.

Dandelion Garden. Grow a weed garden of dandelions—a great nervine, good for soothing the nervous system.

THE COMMON DANDELION IS THE HEALING NERVINE OF THE 21ST CENTURY

What's Growing on Here?
Turning Over the Garden Beds

Purpose: To turn over the soil in preparation for planting, to learn what is living in the soil, and to document findings.

Discovery Questions: What do we need to do to prepare the soil for planting after the beds are constructed? Who is currently living in our garden soil?

Working Tools: Spading forks, shovels, rototiller for large spaces, buckets for collecting rocks, garden bow (i.e., metal) rakes, and hoes.

Learning Tools: Bug boxes, hand lenses, field guides to local insects, paper, pencils, clipboards, and cups.

TURN THE SOIL

Important note: Because this activity involves the use of a sharp spading fork, all participants must wear sturdy footwear for protection—boots are optimal.

1. Starting in center of bed, take spading fork or shovel and dig down approximately eight to 12 inches, depending on the depth of the bed. Turn the soil over completely.
2. Continuing out to the edges of the bed, repeat this procedure until the entire bed area has been tilled.
3. Break up the large clods of soil into small particles. Using a spading fork, shake each clod vigorously until it breaks up and falls through the tines.
4. Remove large rocks and stones from soil. Reserve rocks in a bucket.
5. Continue turning and breaking up the soil in this fashion until all the beds have soil of the same fine consistency.

Extensions:

Rock Contest. How many rocks can you collect in 10 minutes? Who has the most rocks? Who has the biggest and the smallest rock? How many different colored rocks do we have? What kinds of rocks are these—sedimentary, metamorphic, igneous?

Rock Decoration. Use the rocks to make sculptures, to line the beds, to put in walkways. Make a rock garden.

DISCOVER WHO IS LIVING IN THE SOIL

This exercise should be done in conjunction with "Turn the Soil" above.

1. As you are turning over the soil, be on the lookout for any moving creatures: earthworms, spiders, soil beetles, insect larvae, etc.
2. Place any creature you find in bug boxes or cups.
3. Use field guides to identify your specimens.
4. Record findings in a notebook. Draw diagrams. Create your own Bug Book.
5. Return the living creatures back to their home in the soil.

Extensions:

Bug Book. Throughout the growing season, observe the insects that live in your garden community. Who are they? How have they changed over the season? Are they beneficial or harmful insects to your garden plants?

Insect Collection. If they are beneficial, what kinds of habitat will keep them in the garden? If they are harmful, how much damage are they doing? Document your findings. For older children, begin an insect collection. How can you safely control them?

In your Bug Book, create a separate guide that describes beneficial and harmful insects in your garden. Include diagrams, descriptions, time of season found, the plants where the insects are found, and methods of attracting or controlling. For more information about insects, consult your local agriculture extension office (usually located at a state university). Invite a local entomologist to help.

Let the Planting Begin!
Planting the Garden Beds

Purpose: To learn the concepts of proper plant spacing and companion planting, to create and use a garden map, and to plant the beds with new seeds and transplants.

Discovery Questions: How do we map out the location of the plants to be grown in the garden? How do we determine and map out the locations and spacing of the plants to be grown in the garden?

Working Tools: Seeds, labels, transplants, string (to mark rows), gardening rake, hose and/or watering can with a watering rose on the spout, compost (optional), and a base map of your garden.

Learning Tools: Tracing paper, pencils, notebooks, colored pencils, crayons, seed catalogues for reference, general plant reference texts, and a companion planting guide.

MAKING A GARDEN MAP

1. Place tracing paper over the garden base map created in Chapter Four. Check seed packets of the transplants and seeds, and calculate the proper spacing for each plant.
2. Mark on the tracing paper where you will place each plant according to its packet's spacing specifications. Create a symbol for each plant—a circle for tomatoes, a triangle for carrots, etc.

Factors to consider:

✔ Use a companion planting guide to determine which plants grow well together. The book *Carrots Love Tomatoes* by Louise Riotte is especially useful.

✔ In subsequent years, consider what has already been planted in each bed, so that the same plants are not put in the same spot year after year. Failure to rotate plants can degrade the soil and encourage plant-specific pests and diseases.

✔ Take note of the cardinal directions in planning your garden, so that taller plants do not over-shadow sun-loving plants. Planting tomatoes on the south or west side of the garden will make growing difficult for plants like beans or broccoli, which need plenty of sunlight.

Extensions:

A Special Map. Create a color-coded garden map. Enlarge and laminate it for display at the site.

The Garden Yearbook. Start a Garden Yearbook beginning with the color-coded garden map. As the garden grows, keep track of germination dates, harvest dates, rainfall totals, and other meteorological data. Include journal entries and reflections, as well as photos and drawings.

PLANTING SEEDS AND TRANSPLANTS

1. Collect all the seeds and transplants you plan to plant.
2. Use your garden map to plant the seeds and transplants in the appropriate areas.
   Important note: To prevent wilting, transplants should be planted either later in the day when the sun is not at its strongest, or on an overcast day.
3. Label each row of seeds and seedlings with the date started and the name of the plant.
4. After planting, water the rows thoroughly! For added fertility, use fish emulsion (available at local feed stores) or spirulina (available at natural food stores).
   Important note: You may "top-dress" the transplants with compost by dribbling a circle of compost around the young plant.
5. Wait and watch.
6. Weed, water, thin, and mulch.

The Garden Private Eye
Starting a Garden Journal

Purpose: To develop the skills for detecting changes in the garden ecosystem; to develop a method for taking detailed note of these changes; to gain a deeper understanding of the plants, insects, and animals living in the garden and their relationship to one another.

Discovery Question: How do we observe and record the changes that happen in our garden throughout the season?

Working Tools: The five senses.

Learning Tools: Clipboards, paper, pencils, notebooks, colored pencils, crayons, magnifying lenses, general plant and insect reference texts.

Procedure:

1. Each child, or group of two or three, adopts a garden bed to observe throughout the season.
2. Twice a week, using the Data Sheet on the following page (or one you design yourself), children record their observations of the plants growing in their adopted garden bed. The data sheet can be copied so that each plant variety has its own sheet. All of the red oak leaf lettuce would have one data sheet, for example, and black-seeded Simpson, another. All plants of each variety should be observed on every visit; but each time, only draw a picture of one plant of each variety.
3. Encourage students to write down discussion questions each time.
4. Reassemble as a large group to compare notes, discuss observations, and answer questions. These sheets can be the foundation for a gardening journal for children.

Garden Journal Data Sheet

To track the growth of your garden plants through the growing season.

Plant Name: _____

Date Sowed (or set out): _____ Date Germinated: _____ Date Harvested: _____

On separate sheets:
a) Draw a picture of the seedling.
b) Create a seedling guide featuring all your plants at the early seedling stage.
c) Draw a weekly picture of the plant.

Plant characteristics (how they look): _____

_____

_____

_____

Describe weeds near plants (write about and/or describe, draw each weed type): _____

_____

_____

_____

Describe insects near plants (write, draw): _____

_____

_____

_____

Other observations (soil condition, air temperature): _____

_____

_____

_____

Notes: _____

_____

_____

_____

Questions: _____

_____

_____

_____

_____

Developing a Specialty Food Product

For ambitious entrepreneurs, growing and marketing a specialty food product is an exciting project to pursue in the community garden. If planned properly, a specialty food product can involve children in every aspect of the food cycle—growing, processing, packaging, field-testing, and marketing—and provide a clear goal to work toward.

Divide the process into three distinct steps—growing the ingredients, processing and packaging, and marketing and distributing the finished product.

GROWING THE INGREDIENTS

Which vegetables and herbs you grow obviously depends on the specialty food product that you decide to develop. Every food item that goes into the end product need not be grown on site or even locally in order to market it as a locally made food product. Some herbs and most spices, for example, are rather difficult to grow in cooler climates.

*Key questions for the
garden planning process:*

- What specialty food product do we want to produce?
- What ingredients are needed for our specialty food product?
- What ingredients do we want to grow in the garden?
- What quantity do we want to produce?
- How many plants do we need to produce the quantity desired?

PROCESSING AND PACKAGING

Once the vegetables and herbs for the specialty food product have been harvested from the garden, they must be cleaned and prepared for packaging. Each vegetable or herb must be treated in a special way to maintain its quality. Determine the best way to preserve each ingredient you use in your product. Again, consult local food growers and processors.

*Key questions for planning
post harvest activities:*

- What methods of cleaning are necessary for each vegetable or herb prior to storage?
- Which vegetables or herbs need to be dried, frozen, blanched, remain unwashed, refrigerated, put in sawdust, etc.?
- What storage facility and packaging method are necessary for each vegetable or herb?

MARKETING AND DISTRIBUTION OF THE FINISHED PRODUCT

Designing a label and advertising for the product provides opportunities for children to use the creative arts. Be sure to dream up a catchy name for your product using children's input. Look at existing products similar to yours and study the labels for ideas.

Remember to include the nutritional content of the food on the label. One gardening team even showed how the ingredients fit on the USDA Food Guide Pyramid.

*Key questions for packaging,
marketing, and distribution:*

- What type of packaging will maintain the quality of the product?
- What type of packaging will be the most environmentally friendly?
- What type of packaging will most effectively display the product?
- Who is the target market?
- What are the best methods to reach the target market?

- What sales information is needed to educate the target market?
- What messages and information should be included on the product label?
- How much can we charge for the product?

OTHER IMPORTANT FACTORS TO CONSIDER

USDA rules and regulations that govern the packaging and sale of farm products are strict. Generally, food processing must be done in an inspected and approved kitchen environment. The jars, bottles, or containers in which the food is packaged must be completely sanitized. Contact the USDA office in your state's capital for the official guidelines.

Be sure to factor in the cost of containers in pricing your product.

Start small. You may not be able to pull off a large operation the first time around. The initial year is often a time for experimenting with different recipes, test marketing foods on friends and family, and later settling on a product that can be produced the following year. Use this first year for advanced publicity for launching the specialty food product in year two.

SOME IDEAS FOR A SPECIALTY FOOD PRODUCT

- *Pizza Sauce:* Experiment with different combinations of herbs mixed in with tomato sauce. Broccoli pizza sauce could be a surprise favorite.
- *Chili:* Mix together your own unique batch of beans, peppers, tomatoes, and culinary herbs. Add in onions and favorite spices, too. Collect and compare recipes from home.
- *Salsa:* Innovate from recipes in cookbooks, or ask a local restaurant manager.
- *Pesto:* Use dill or cilantro from the garden; get an old recipe from Grandma.
- *Pickles:* See page 74 for pickled beans recipe.
- *Salad Dressing:* Use your own herb mix from the garden.

6

Growing Mysteries: Activities for Summer

School's out, sprinklers are on, and weeds are growing like there's no tomorrow. It's summer—the time when plants do most of their growing, and when people are on the go. With the onset of hot weather, the demands of the garden shift from such labor-intensive activities as breaking up soil and building raised beds, to lighter everyday chores, such as thinning, mulching, and weeding. Having a successful harvest means bringing people together around the growing bounty of crops. But summertime is also playtime! Weaving laughter, leisure, and enjoyment into the summer gardening program is one way to insure that kids will come back week after week.

This chapter includes horticultural activities that can be done throughout the summer, including watering, mulching, and composting. Continue the weeding and insect activities from Chapter Five as well. Other activities are designed to involve children in play and imaginative theater.

Brown Bag Botany is a popular exercise in which children try to guess which parts of a plant various common foods come from. (For example, which part of the plant are onions? Hint: They're not roots.) An extension to the activity, called Around the World, is another food-plant matching game that creatively mixes learning and play.

Garden theater comes to life with the first-ever Insect Opera, a wildly inventive arts activity dreamt up by music teacher Erik Nielsen of Brookfield, Vermont. Children of all ages take on the identities of garden insects while conducting research into the habitats, habits, anatomy, and sounds of their insect alter egos. After making appropriate costumes and props, and practicing their insect's song, the group of bugs create an improvised natural garden symphony.

Another activity in the chapter, Eating the Food Guide Pyramid, is a nutrition exercise that involves a field trip to the local farmers' market to purchase locally grown foods and match them to the food groups in the USDA Food Guide Pyramid.

All these activities will clearly show children that a gardening program involves far more than planting seeds and harvesting vegetables and will explore all aspects of a community's food cycle in ways that are interesting and fun.

THINGS TO DO IN THE SUMMER GARDEN (BESIDES WEEDING)

read
sketch
listen
sing
graze
play
make herb necklaces and crowns
smell the flowers
observe the insects
write a poem
think
put on a play
hold a community meal
cook
teach
nap
have a tea party
paint

Thirst Quenchers
Watering the Garden

Purpose: To keep plants adequately watered during the growing season.

Discovery Question: How do we insure our garden has enough water throughout the growing season?

Working Tools: Hoses, sprinkler (oscillating), watering wand, soaker hoses, and nozzle with adjustable water flows.

Learning Tools: Rain gauge, paper, and pencils.

Important note: Keeping the garden watered during the hot summer months is extremely important. Inadequate water is one of the most common reasons why gardens fail.

Procedure:

1. Set up a rain gauge to measure the amount of rainfall each week. To make your own rain gauge, take a clear glass jar and mark off inches on the outside. Set it in the garden away from buildings or trees that might distort the readings. A rain gauge can also be purchased at any garden supply center. Check the rain gauge every morning at approximately the same time, and record findings in a logbook. Empty the water out each morning.

2. As a general rule, growing plants need one inch of water per week to mature properly. If your rain gauge measures less than one inch of rain per week, watering will be necessary. Often, even when the rainfall totals an inch per week, watering is still necessary because of other weather conditions such as high temperatures, high winds, lots of sun, and low humidity—anything that could dry out the soil. Check plants and feel the soil daily to test for dryness. Pay attention to the plants—are they drooping?

3. To water plants, use any of the tools listed above. For large gardens, a sprinkler is most convenient. Water thoroughly.

4. To check if you have watered enough, use the finger test. Poke your index finger all the way into the soil. If the soil feels moist along the entire

length of your finger, you have watered enough. If not, keep watering. The goal is to keep the soil consistently moist to a depth of three inches.

Extensions:

Water, Rain, and Weather.

1. Make a weather station: A small lean-to to record weather data can be used year round. Instruments to include are a min./max. thermometer, wind gauge, rain gauge, barometer, and hydrometer. Make a daily weather logbook. Check instruments and record data at the same time every day. This creates a good weather record from year to year. Make charts and graphs, tracking temperature changes, rainfall levels, etc. This develops great math skills.

2. Interview a weather forecaster from a local TV or radio station. Visit the area National Weather Bureau station.

We Got It Covered
Mulching the Garden

Mulching is the process of covering the soil with materials that will slow the evaporation of water, inhibit weed growth, and keep the soil cool.

Purpose: To conserve moisture, keep weeds down, and keep the soil cool in mid-summer.

Discovery Question: How do we reduce the amount of watering and weeding needed during the growing season?

Materials: Organic mulches—bark mulch, wood chips, composted leaves, sawdust, grass clippings, straw, and cocoa mulch; Inorganic mulches—newspaper, cardboard, old rugs, and plastic.

Procedure:

1. Thoroughly weed all of the garden beds that are to be mulched.
2. Carefully place the mulching material around your plants. Completely cover the soil all around the plants, making sure the mulch does not touch the stems of the plants. Generally, organic mulches should be two to four inches deep for best results.
3. Keep track of the mulch levels through the course of the season. The organic mulches will break down eventually, and will need to be replenished periodically (about every four weeks) in order to keep the mulch depth at two to four inches.

Extension:

Comparing Mulches. Compare organic versus inorganic mulch (i.e., grass clippings versus cocoa mulch). Set up different test plots in the garden to test the effectiveness of various mulches. Place the different mulches around the same type of plants. Place wood chips around tomatoes in one bed, and cardboard around tomatoes in another. Compare the results.

Factors to test include: effectiveness in inhibiting weeds, promoting plant growth, and preventing fungal diseases and pests, and making cost comparisons.

After a year, compare soils that used different mulches to see if the soil nutrient content is the same or different.

Check underneath the mulches to see which creatures are living off the different kinds of mulches. Are they different? How? Why? Record your findings in the Garden Log Book.

Brown Bag Botany
Learning about Edible Plant Parts

Purpose: To introduce students to the edible parts of plants, and to help students identify the nutritional qualities of different plant parts.

Materials: Large brown paper bag, labels identifying each of the plant parts listed, an assortment of foods, including a variety of plant part products such as

- *Roots*: carrots, beets, tapioca
- *Stems*: celery, potatoes, sugar
- *Leaves*: tea, lettuce, spinach, onion
- *Flowers*: chamomile tea, nasturtiums
- *Buds*: broccoli, brussel sprouts
- *Fruit*: cucumber, pepper, pizza sauce, catsup
- *Seeds*: alfalfa sprouts, bread, spaghetti, coffee, cereal, oatmeal, rice

Procedure:

1. Set up stations with a label or sign for each plant.
2. Fill the paper bag with an assortment of edible foods from each of the plant-part categories above.
3. In teams of two, students pull foods out of the bag and try to match their foods with the corresponding plant parts. Lettuce, for example, would be placed in the station marked "leaves."
4. When everyone has had a turn, review and critique.

Plant Part Chart

PART	DESCRIPTION/DEFINITION	EXAMPLES
Root	Usually forms below ground, acts as an anchor for the plant, absorbs water and minerals, and provides physical support and food storage.	daikon, burdock, tapioca, carrots
Stem	Provides support for the buds and leaves, and gives the plant its form. Serves as a conduit for water, minerals, gases, and sugars.	potatoes
Bud	An undeveloped shoot from which leaves or flowers grow. A flower bud includes a short stem with embryonic flower parts.	broccoli, artichokes, brussel sprouts
Leaf	The part of the plant involved in photosynthesis and transpiration. Leaves include: stoma, guard cells, epidermis, cuticles, veins, chlorophyll, and chloroplasts.	parsley, onions, celery, lettuce, mint, chives, garlic, tea
Flower	The structure that contains the organs for sexual reproduction. Also, the site where pollination occurs.	nasturtiums, chamomile, hibiscus
Seed	Fertilized ovules grow and swell to form seeds after pollination has occurred. A seed contains an embryo (which has all the necessary genetic information to create a new plant), an endosperm (the food required to sustain early growth), and a seed coat (which protects the seed from disease).	shell peas, wheat products, oats, cocoa, peanut butter, corn starch, coffee
Fruit	The enlarged ovary surrounding the newly developed seed is the true fruit of the plant. The fruit holds and protects the seed.	pumpkins, tomatoes, vanilla, snap peas, green beans, avocados, peaches, grapes

Extensions:

1. This activity leads to a discussion about the function of each plant part and the importance of these different parts as nutrients for humans. Make a list of the foods students have recently eaten. Which ones are from plants? What part of the plant was used?

2. How else do humans use different plant parts? Perfumes, dyes, fabrics, cleansers, shampoos, etc.

3. Around the World: The Plant Parts Guessing Game. The object of the game is for a player to work her way "around the world," moving around the circle to return to her seat. The first one to do so is the winner.
   a. All the children sit in a circle. One child stands behind one of the children sitting in the circle.
   b. The facilitator names a food, and the children yell out the plant part that it comes from.
   c. If the standing player guesses first, she gets to move clockwise around the circle to stand behind the next student. If the standing student guesses incorrectly, she changes places with the child she is standing behind.
   d. If a seated player guesses the correct plant part first, that player stands, and the standing child sits in that empty place.

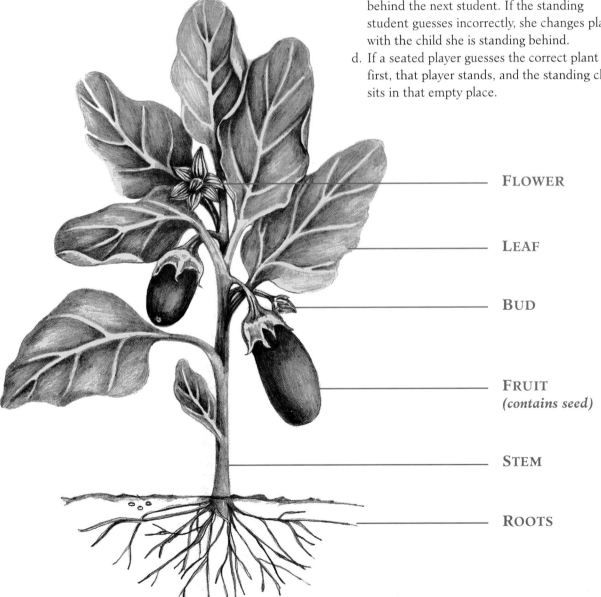

FLOWER

LEAF

BUD

FRUIT
(contains seed)

STEM

ROOTS

What's Bugging You?
Performing an Insect Opera

Pioneered by Erik Nielsen, music teacher at the Waits River Valley School in Vermont.

Purpose: To combine musical and theatrical skills with scientific knowledge about the anatomy, habits, and life cycle of both "harmful" and "beneficial" insects (and the plants that nourish and host them) to create an opera using vocal and instrumental music, movement, costumes, and sets.

Discovery Question: How can we creatively demonstrate our knowledge of the insect world using our artistic skills?

Materials: Natural and prefabricated materials for costumes, sets, and all the props for recreating a garden on stage.

"To bee or not to bee"

Procedure:

1. Students create a simple narrative describing any aspect of the insect world that they would like to depict: a basic predator-prey relationship involving insects in the garden; or a symbiotic relationship. Any combination of these will do, or create something entirely different.
2. Add elaborate variations to the story. Other insects that are harmful to plant life could appear, or the garden could be sprayed with insecticide, etc.
3. Students choose which insect or plant to play, and make costumes, detailing the exact anatomy of the insect or plant.
4. Through improvisation, students make up their own movements, dialogue (if desired), dance, and music. They can do this in small groups, or individually by writing, brainstorming, or acting it out.
5. Students develop appropriate scenery, using both natural and prefabricated arts materials.
6. Rehearse, rehearse, rehearse! Improve the script each time. Add where possible, cut where appropriate.
7. Perform for different types of audiences: students, parents, community groups, seniors, etc.

The variations on this activity are virtually limitless—the honeybee-rose love duet, the march of the mantis, decomposing with plants or getting down and dirty with the compost pile, dance of the damselfly, or the squash bug samba—to name just a few. Like most operas, this could contain choruses, duets, and solos, though this is completely up to the performers. For younger children (grades K–2), the process can be simplified so that insect sound choruses may take the place of songs with words, and instrumental and movement demands can be simplified.

Extension:

Insect Songs. Developing and performing Insect Songs can be the most creative part of The Insect Opera. The purpose of this activity is to combine knowledge of insects and their behaviors with composing the melody (and words, where appropriate) of a series of songs about specific insects. These can be used as choral pieces or solos in The Insect Opera.

Procedure:

1. Brainstorm a list of insects.
2. Choose several insects from the list.
3. Determine a basic story line then break into small groups.
4. The small groups can proceed as they see fit. Each group can practice songs of one insect, or individuals within each group can assume the identity of separate insects, or an entirely different procedure can be agreed upon.
5. Revise and refine ideas of each group into song texts.
6. Create, refine, and practice a melody for each song.
7. Add musical instruments to the symphony as appropriate.
8. Determine the exact sequence of songs and movements.
9. Add creative movement, dance.
10. Practice repeatedly.
11. Perform for the masses.

The wonderful thing about a project like this is that there is something for just about every student: the observer of nature, the visual artist, the ham, the singer, the rhymer, the drummer, the carpenter, the costumer can each have an important role in the creation and development of the opera. Although not all ideas will be used, everyone's input and skills are important, and the process will teach children about problem solving and group decision-making. It is also important for children to observe several teachers working cooperatively on the project, and to see how all areas of knowledge can fit together.

The Bold and Beautiful
Introducing Children to Edible Flowers

We grow flowers for their beautiful colors, shapes, and fragrances. We don't, however, usually think of growing them for food. But in fact, many flowers are delicious when added to salads and sandwiches, candied, used in flavored vinegars, or set to float in soups or ice tea.

Purpose: To learn how to prepare edible flowers.

Discovery Question: Which flowers are edible? How can they be prepared?

CARE OF EDIBLE FLOWERS

Plant the flower seeds in planting containers, and put plastic wrap over the tops. Place pots on a sunny windowsill, and check them every day. Lift the plastic and feel the soil. If it's dry, mist it gently. When the seeds germinate, remove the plastic wrap. Seeds should germinate in seven to 10 days.

You can tell if plants need water while they are growing by sticking your finger into the soil. If the soil is dry below the surface, it is time to water. Pour in enough water so that it runs out the bottom of the pot.

About two weeks after the seeds have germinated, fertilize the plants with a very diluted solution of fertilizer. Marigolds and nasturtiums don't need much fertilizer.

Transplant to the garden when ready. With plenty of sunshine, water, and TLC, plants should flower, and the children can eat the blooms. While waiting for the nasturtiums to flower, try eating some leaves. Mix up a salad of greens and flowers, or make up one of the following recipes.

FLORAL VINEGARS

Use cider or wine vinegar as a base. Gently crush freshly picked blossoms and herbs, and loosely fill a jar. Add lukewarm vinegar to fill the jar. Cap with an acid-proof lid. Set the jar in a sunny window, and shake daily for two weeks. After two weeks, taste. If you want a stronger flavor, strain the vinegar, and repeat the process with fresh herbs and blossoms. To store, strain through cheesecloth, or leave as is. For visual appeal, add fresh (uncrushed) blossoms and herbs. Label. Use in salad dressings, marinades, gravies, and sauces.

Try these combinations:

- **1 part lavender flowers to 1 part lemon verbena**
- **1 part lavender flowers to 3 parts rose petals**

Experiment with your own combinations of edible flowers and your favorite herbs.

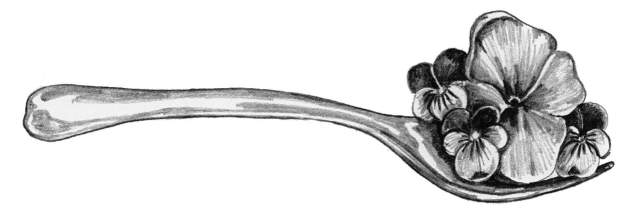

Rose Petal Jam

- **1 lb. heavily scented red or pink rose petals**
- **2 cups water**
- **2¹/₂ cups superfine sugar**
- **juice of 2 lemons**
- **1 tbsp. rosewater**

1. Remove the bitter white base from each petal. Rinse and drain the petals.
2. Bring the water to a boil in a large, heavy saucepan. Reduce heat to simmer, then add the rose petals. The mixture will froth up considerably, so do not fill the pan more than half full. Simmer gently for five minutes until the petals are soft.
3. Add sugar and lemon juice. Bring back to a boil and simmer for about 30 minutes, stirring until the sugar has dissolved and the mixture begins to thicken. Add the rosewater.
4. Let the mixture boil. When the bubbles have turned to foam, remove pan from heat, and spoon out a little bit of the mixture. Put it in a saucer, let cool, then push the surface. If it wrinkles, it is ready. If no wrinkles appear, return to heat and cook longer, testing again when the bubbles become foamy.
5. Allow the jam to cool slightly, then pour into sterilized jars, seal, and label.

Candied Blossoms

- **Fresh blossoms, carefully washed and well drained**
- **1 egg white, beaten until frothy**
- **Superfine sugar**

Dip the blossoms in the egg white. Hold the blossoms over a plate or bowl while you sprinkle them with sugar. Make sure you coat all surfaces. Place the blossoms on waxed paper, and let them dry in a warm place for two days. You may use these to decorate cookies or cakes. To store, put in a tightly sealed glass jar with waxed paper placed between layers of the flowers. Have fun growing and eating!

Common Plants with Edible Flowers

The first name is the plant's Latin name, followed by its common name.

Important note: Never eat flowers that may have been sprayed. Never eat any flower unless you know what plant it is from and that it is safe to eat.

Alcea, hollyhock
Allium, chives and garlic chives
Anethum, dill
Begonia, tuberous begonia
Borago, borage
Brassica, mustard
Calendula, also known as pot marigold
Citrus, lemon and orange
Cucurbita, squash
Dianthus, carnation
Gladiolus
Hemerocallis, daylily (buds)
Lavandula, lavender
Matricaria, German chamomile
Monarda, bee balm
Ocimum, basil
Origanum, oregano and marjoram
Pelargonium, scented-leaved geraniums (these are not common window-box geraniums)
Phaseolus, beans
Pisum, peas
Rosa, roses
Salvia, sage and pineapple sage
Syringa, lilac
Tagetes, marigold, especially signet marigold (*T. tenuifolia*)
Thymus, thyme
Tulipa, tulip
Viola, Johnny-jump-up, pansy, and violet

Eating the Food Guide Pyramid
Complete Nutrition at the Farmers' Market

Purpose: To purchase locally produced foods at the farmers' market and match them to the Food Guide Pyramid.

Discovery Question: What locally produced foods purchased at the farmers' market match up with the USDA Food Guide Pyramid?

Materials: USDA Food Guide Pyramid, "Farm-to-Family Coupons" (if available) obtained from a local social and human services office.

Procedure:

1. Familiarize children with the food groups in the Food Guide Pyramid. The older children who already know the Pyramid can team up with younger ones and tutor them for five to 10 minutes. Divide the group into teams. Quiz each team by asking them to match a food item with the appropriate food group on the Pyramid.

2. Plan a field trip to the local farmers' market. Meet at a convenient location on or near the market grounds. Establish this spot as Home Base.

3. Every team draws a picture of the Food Guide Pyramid on the ground near Home Base. Use sticks to draw in the dirt or to lay out on the grass; use chalk to draw on the sidewalk.

4. Each two-person team must purchase foods from every food group in the Pyramid. If your state has "Farm-to-Family Coupons," use those. If funds are available, each team should be able to fill out the Pyramid with modest food purchases totaling no more than seven dollars.

5. As the foods are bought, children return to their own Pyramids and place their purchases in the corresponding food groups.

6. When all the Pyramids, are filled, each group gives a presentation on what was purchased, how much it cost, and how much change is left over. Take a photo of each team standing beside its completed Pyramid.

7. After the presentations, everyone gets to eat their Pyramid.

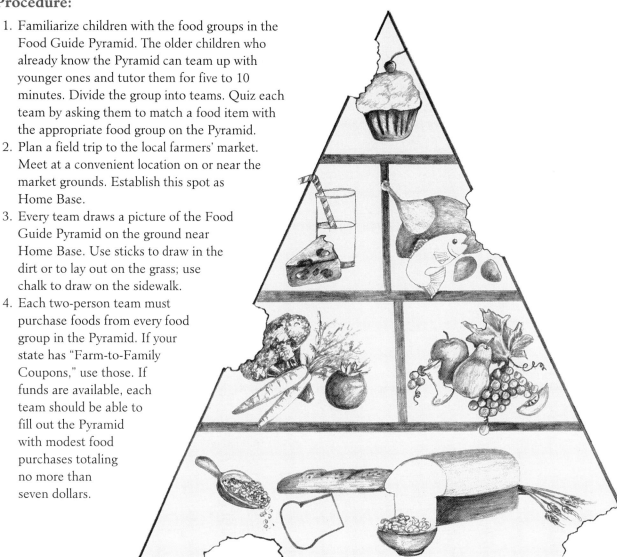

What Goes Around Comes Around
Making a Compost Cake

Purpose: To learn the basics of making nutrient-rich material to add to garden soil. The main objectives of this activity are:

- to create a mini compost pile
- to explore the components of a compost pile
- to learn what happens to compost over time
- to investigate finished compost
- to construct a compost system for your garden

Discovery Question: How do we transform organic garden waste into useful material for growing plants?

Working Tools: Two five-gallon buckets, grass clippings, leaves, straw, weeds, soil, a bucket of water, a bucket of finished compost.

Learning Tools: Fabrics, paper plates, paper bags, yarn, string, scissors, glue, cardboard, crayons, water colors, markers, masking/duct tape, paper punch, sticks.

Background Information: Composting is the process of transforming materials such as weeds, grass, roots, and kitchen scraps. When these materials are piled into a confined space, they break down quickly, forming a fine soil-like substance that is rich in nutrients, improves soil structure, and helps protect plants against certain diseases.

For Decomposition Drama have a bucket of finished compost on hand. If your garden does not have any compost yet, check with a local gardener or a community compost project.

MAKING A COMPOST CAKE

1. Make individual piles of grass clippings, leaves, straw, weeds, and soil. These and the bucket of water are the ingredients for your compost. How are they the same? How are they different? What are their colors? Smells?
2. Poke drainage holes in the bottom of the empty five-gallon bucket. In the bottom of the bucket, place a brown layer of leaves and straw. Shovel a small amount of soil over the brown layer.
3. Add a layer of watery green materials such as grass clippings and weeds. Shovel a small amount of soil over the green layer.
4. Continue alternating brown layers and green layers until all the materials are used. Mix a shovelful or two of soil on top of each layer as you go.
5. Moisten the contents of the bucket to the dampness of a wrung-out sponge.
6. Wait two weeks.

DECOMPOSITION DRAMA

Put together a dramatization of what is happening to your mini compost pile over a two-week period.

1. Create costumes, masks, and props depicting the sun, the moon, the stars, rain, clouds, and compost pile ingredients (before and after).
2. Demonstrate the passing of time from day to night and night to day—sun rise and set, moon rise and set, clouds roll in, rain falls, etc. Repeat several times.
3. As time passes, the kids portraying the compost pile ingredients act out what is happening to them.
4. After two weeks have passed, the compost is finished. Now what do you think has happened to our compost?
5. Show participants the finished bucket of compost.

Wormley's Magic Waste-to-Riches
Making Compost in Two Weeks

Here's a neat magic trick children can perform in their own neighborhood or schoolyard garden, turning weeds and kitchen waste into brown gold in two weeks.

Magic Trick Preparation: Every great magician knows that the success of each trick depends on thorough preparation.

To prepare for this 14-day trick, it is necessary to build a triple-bin compost system out of old wooden recycled pallets as shown on page 39. Find a flat, shaded area for the compost bins that is close to the garden. The site should be four feet by 12 feet and can be up against a fence or wall.

Compost Layering Materials: Bale of hay or straw; lots and lots of food scraps from the kitchen (three 30-gallon garbage cans are ideal); lots and lots of grass clippings (six garbage bags); if available, garden hose with a spray nozzle; cubic yard of topsoil (from the garden, or from the ground under the compost bin); five-gallon bucket of animal manure (horse, goat, chicken) or commercial bonemeal, bloodmeal, and compost starter.

Tools: Several five-gallon buckets; garden spade, shovels, compost fork, staple gun and staples (or three-quarter-inch metal staples and hammer), sledgehammer, crowbar, saw, wire cutters, compost thermometer, clipboard and paper, and magic wand.

Procedure:

1. Excavate one foot of soil from the bases of all the bins, and pile it off to the left.
2. A team of children takes five-gallon buckets to their homes and into the community to collect organic kitchen food scraps. (These food scraps should be uncooked and without any oil, animal grease and/or fats.) Children can explain, "We're doing a magic trick and collecting food scraps to turn into gold. Please put your uncooked food scraps and coffee grounds in this bucket for us to pick up next week."

3. The children collect the five-gallon buckets that are filled with food scraps, and dump them into the large 30-gallon cans for easy storage. Once all three containers are full, and bags of grass clippings are collected, the trick can begin.

THE MAGIC TRICK BEGINS

Children dress up in their most mysterious and magical outfits—top hats and capes, wands and scarves. Announce to all the neighbors that a magic show will begin at the garden at a particular time and date.

The children can recite, together or individually, some version of the following:

Ladies and Gentlemen,

You are about to witness the most astonishing disappearing act to ever happen in this community. Right here in front of your very eyes, we will take all of your yukkiest food scraps—your coffee grinds and onion skins, your potato peels and pea husks, your apple cores and banana peels—and transform them into organic gold, using secret, never-before-seen creatures, invisible to the naked human eye—microorganisms—otherwise known as decomposers! All of this, in less than two weeks!

Come see for yourself! Step right up! Step right up! Let's have a show of hands here—how many people believe that this amazing feat can be pulled off by a small group of kids?

As this is being recited, children are layering the compost pile in the first bin, chanting the magic words: "Hay, water, food, soil. Hay, water, food, soil." This is the secret formula for layering the magic compost: one layer of hay on the bottom is followed by a light misting of water, then a layer of "food" (manure, green grass clippings, or food scraps) topped by a layer of soil; repeat several times until the pile is three feet high.

Begin with a four-inch layer of hay as a base. Next, lightly spray water from a hose to cover the hay. Add some manure or a mix of bonemeal, bloodmeal, and compost starter. Then sprinkle a thin layer of soil over the entire pile. Begin the next cycle of hay/water/food/soil with another four-inch layer of hay. Sprinkle with water, then add two to four inches of grass clippings and a couple inches of soil. On a clipboard, keep track of all the layers and what goes on each layer. Wait to add kitchen food scraps on the food layer until after repeating the hay/water/food/soil cycle three times.

When the pile is three feet high, wave magic wands over the pile, recite a final incantation, and invite friends and neighbors to return in two weeks to witness the transformation.

For Compost Magicians Only
(All Others: Do Not Read!)

The Secret to the Trick:

As the magician, you are really a farmer of hidden microorganisms that turn food wastes into brown gold, or nutrient-rich fertilizer, which, in turn, nourishes strong and healthy plants. The compost described here is a near-perfect mix of carbohydrates (hay and leaves), protein (green grass, green leaves, and food scraps), a sprinkling of water, and plenty of air. As long as you layer these ingredients, the secret microorganisms will eat the food waste, heat up the pile, and multiply like crazy.

The sleight of hand you must perform in order to pull off this magic trick is this: Every three to five days, the compost pile must be completely turned over from one bin to the other. By doing so you are allowing the compost to "breathe," i.e., to receive enough oxygen for the microorganisms to eat, heat, and multiply.

The most important element that allows these microorganisms to continue eating, heating, and multiplying is air. Over the first three to five days, your pile will continue to heat from 120 to 150 degrees. As soon as the temperature drops, the pile must be turned over into the next bin, or the microorganisms will slow down. When the pile is turned into the next bin and exposed to fresh air, the temperature will begin to climb again.

Therefore, it is important to keep close watch on your compost thermometer, and record the temperature every day. As soon as the temperature begins to drop, turn the compost over into the next bin. In two weeks—*voila!*—you have brown gold.

7

Harvesting Discoveries: Activities for Fall

The fall is a wonderful time to be in the garden for fun and adventure, and for discovery and hands-on learning. The joy of reaping the harvest after a season of labors is equaled only by the excitement of learning the intimate interconnections in nature through careful exploration of your garden in full bloom. This chapter describes the basic horticultural activities to complete in the fall, from harvest to seed saving to putting food by, and cover cropping; and it details several activities that students can pursue in the garden, with a special emphasis on nutrition.

This chapter contains clear, step-by-step directions for a wide range of practical post-harvest activities, including: saving seeds, making dilled pickles and beans, making pesto pizza, and freezing vegetables. Another activity offers directions for putting the garden to bed after it has been thoroughly gleaned. Others highlight the fun and creative things that can be done around harvest time, such as: making a vegetable book based on the five senses, creating jewelry out of vegetables, developing an advertising campaign for favorite vegetables, making a community harvest cookbook, and holding a community celebration in the garden.

If you would like to share any of your favorite garden activities with children from the spring, summer, fall, or winter, send them along, and we'll include them in the next edition of *Digging Deeper*.

Mail to: Food Works, 64 Main Street, Montpelier, Vermont 05602; or e-mail: <rootsnet@plainfield.bypass.com>.

The fall is by no means the only time to harvest crops planted in the spring. The first harvest of lettuce, for example, can often come in June if seedlings are started early enough. The peak of the harvest, however, comes when the weather begins to turn cold. In addition to planning when to harvest which crops, it is also important to create a plan for using and distributing the harvest.

What to Do with the Garden Bounty

- ✔ School lunches and snacks
- ✔ Cooking and baking: zucchini bread, pumpkin cookies, vegetable stir fries, spaghetti sauce, sunflower seeds, etc.
- ✔ Canning: dilly beans, dilled pickles, salsa
- ✔ Freezing: green beans, broccoli, pesto, corn
- ✔ Cold storage: potatoes, carrots, turnips, squash
- ✔ Drying: herbs, tomatoes, flowers
- ✔ Make flower essences
- ✔ Candy flowers
- ✔ Craftmaking: potpourri, wreaths, dried flower arrangements, gourd birdhouses, rattles, creatures
- ✔ Remedies and tinctures: mullein remedy, burdock root, echinacea, plantain leaves, dandelions (roots and leaves), rose hips
- ✔ Compete for awards at county fairs
- ✔ Donate to local soup kitchens, food shelves, and senior centers
- ✔ Give flowers to hospitals, friends, and family
- ✔ Save seeds for next spring's planting
- ✔ Sell produce at a farm stand or farmers' market
- ✔ Photograph, paint, draw, compose stories, poems, and songs
- ✔ Learn nutrition basics
- ✔ Host a community meal

Sense-sational Veggies
Making Your Own Vegetable Book Using the Five Senses

This activity, as well as Carrot Cooking Care, were created by Pamela Brawley of the Waits River Valley School, Vermont.

Purpose: To explore common objects using the five senses of sight, hearing, taste, touch, and smell. To use adjectives that describe the different ways our five senses experience a living thing. To work in teams to create a Sensory Vegetable Book.

Discovery Question: How can we use our five senses to experience a living thing? How can we share those experiences with others?

Materials: Assortment of vegetables, construction paper, glue, and scissors.

Procedure:

1. Explain the purpose of this activity: to use five senses to experience each vegetable, to describe those experiences, and to compile the descriptions in a homemade book.
2. Have the group make a list of the vegetables on hand.
3. Break up the group into teams of five. Each team chooses a vegetable.
4. One person on each team will focus on one of the five senses.
5. Each child examines his or her team's vegetable using his or her assigned sense.
6. Each participant writes one or two sentences describing the vegetable. For example, "A carrot snaps when it is broken in half. When you eat it, it crunches." Teams can make comparisons between vegetables, write poems about their vegetable, etc.
7. Teams should work collaboratively in any way they see fit. They may decide to focus on using one sense together in encountering a vegetable, or they may combine senses and make up a poem about their vegetable.
8. Each team binds its work using string or thread and needle and shares with the rest of the group.
9. The work is collected in a book with a chapter devoted to each vegetable. Chapters can also be divided according to the five senses. Cut out pictures and make drawings of the vegetables to include in the book.

The Inside Story
Flower Dissection

Purpose: To gain an understanding of the parts of a flower and their functions in nature, in the garden, and in the plant itself.

Discovery Questions: How do flowers reproduce? What are the "body parts" of a flower?

Materials: Flowers (florist throwaways, or a variety of different types from the garden), Exacto knives, copies of the illustration below, magnifying glass, tape, and construction paper.

Procedure:

1. Use Exacto knife to dissect a flower. Begin with one straight cut down the center. (Lilies are good flowers to start with because their parts are readily identifiable.)
2. Using the illustration handout, identify key parts along the way (petals, pistil, stamen, etc.).
3. Note the different sizes and shapes of the flower parts. Why do you think nature designed them this way? What do you think each is for? How do you think each enhances or hinders pollination?
4. Create a flower diagram by taping the pieces of your flower on a piece of paper. Label each part and its purpose as you go along.

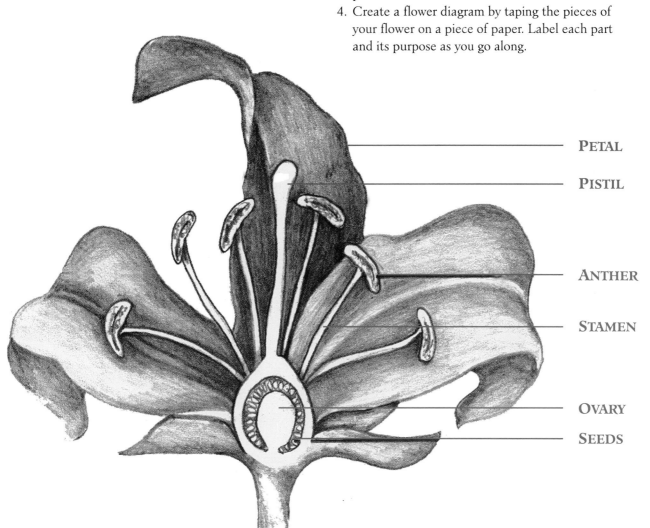

PETAL

PISTIL

ANTHER

STAMEN

OVARY

SEEDS

The Great Seed Rescue
Seed Saving

Purpose: To demonstrate the process of reproducing several different types of plants, including tomatoes, beans, peas, corn, garlic, and potatoes.

Discovery Questions: How can we reproduce favorite plants from our garden?

Materials: Garden vegetables to be used for obtaining seeds—several ears of dried corn, red peppers, several bulbs of garlic, beans, a few potatoes with eyes, four tomatoes, and peas.

Materials for Saving Seeds: String, pushpins, several small glass jars (dark colors work best) with covers, paper towels, knives, and a food mill.

Procedure:

1. Observe plants throughout the season. Select the the strongest, healthiest, and most prolific plants. Mark them with a brightly colored ribbon or tag. You must use plants from open-pollinated, rather than hybrid, seed to yield "true" varieties. Open-pollinated seeds have not been hybridized in a laboratory, but propogated naturally.

   Important note: Many plants will cross-pollinate with a different variety of the same species (for example, from one tomato variety to the next). Students should choose to grow only one variety of any of the following crops to insure that the seed will produce the same variety when grown the following next year.

2. Allow several fruits from your chosen plants to ripen fully on the vine, stalk, or in the ground to enable the seeds to mature. Harvest when ripe.

Saving Tomato Seed:

a. Quarter each tomato and separate the jelly-like substance that contains the seeds. Soak in water overnight.

b. Rinse the seeds once again to remove pulp.

c. Place the seeds on newspaper or cloth in a warm (not hot), dry, dark place and allow to dry hard.

d. Store in an airtight container in a cool, dark place (film canisters, tincture bottles, and seed packets inside a jar with silica packets all work well).

e. Label the jars with the name of the plant, the variety, and the date.

Saving Pepper Seed:

Important note: Peppers cross-pollinate very easily. If more than one variety of pepper is grown in the garden, they must be grown at least 200 feet apart to produce seeds that retain the plants' characteristics.

a. Select good quality peppers that are overripe and starting to wrinkle.

b. Cut peppers in halves or quarters, and remove small brownish seeds from fruit. (If the seeds are still white, they are not fully mature.)

c. Place seeds on newspaper in a warm (not hot), dry, dark place, and allow to dry.

d. Store in an airtight container in a cool, dark place (film canisters, tincture bottles, and seed packets inside a jar with silica packets all work well).

e. Label the jars with the name of the plant, the variety, and the date.

Saving Bean or Pea Seed:

a. Allow the beans or peas to dry on the vine. Select good-quality, large pods.

b. Once dried, harvest, and crack open the pods. Inside, you will find little round balls. These are the seeds.

c. Follow steps c to e, above.

Saving Corn Seed:

a. Allow corn to dry thoroughly on the stalk. Select large, good-quality ears.

b. Choose from one of the following methods:
   • Shuck the corn, and remove the kernels by grasping the cob with two hands and firmly twisting. This should remove the seed from the ear. Place seed in an airtight container.
   • Peel back husks, and tie into bunches. Hang the bunches from string, and use to decorate the classroom until next year's planting.

Saving Garlic Seed:

Although garlic and potatoes are not usually grown from their actual seed, it is fun to utilize these age-old methods for reproducing these plants.

a. Separate the cloves from the bulb (there is no need to peel).

b. Save cloves in a garlic keeper or paper bag until planting. Do not seal in airtight container.

c. A few weeks after the first frost in the fall, plant the cloves about two inches deep with the pointed end up. Mulch the bed to protect from cold.

Saving Potato Seed:

a. Select firm, medium-sized potatoes without signs of disease or rot. Make sure each seed potato has at least two eyes (small bud-like marks where the potato will sprout).

b. Let the potatoes sun cure for two days without getting rained on.

c. Store in an open container in a cold (not freezing) and very damp place until spring. Root cellars work best at 36 degrees with high humidity.

d. Plant potatoes outside in the spring or in containers indoors.

Extensions:

Create a Seed Bank. You may want to develop a collection of heirloom seeds, preserving them for classes and/or generations to come. Be sure to keep an organized list of the names of parent plants and the origins of your original seed. Label your seeds carefully. Seek out other local seed collectors.

Seeds for Sale. Market the seeds you harvest. Place a bunch in an envelope, and design a cover. Refer to other seed packets as examples for your design. Be sure to include pertinent information such as germination rate, planting times and depths, and spacing information. Use the proceeds to fund your garden project.

Mystery History Food Search. Research the origins of your favorite vegetables. How have they come to you? Trace their journey on a map or globe, noting historic events that influenced their journey. In what ways have different cultures utilized these same vegetables?

Contact elders in your community for information about the varieties of seeds they utilized and the seeds' special qualities or characteristics. How did they prepare them? Make a recipe book of your findings.

For food origins, consult *The History of Food*, by Maguelonne Toussaint (Blackwell Publishers, 1992).

Silly Dillies
Making Dilled Pickles and Beans

Purpose: To learn the process of putting food by, and preserving the fruits of your labors. To gain firsthand experience canning foods.

Discovery Question: How do you make dill pickles and beans?

Materials: Apple cider vinegar, water, dill seed or seed heads, cayenne pepper, mustard seeds, garlic cloves, salt, fresh green beans, cucumbers, large pot for brine, medium-sized pot for sterilizing lids and rings, large canning pot and jar rack, quart or pint canning jars, labels and permanent marking pen, tongs, funnel, jar grippers, towels, chop sticks, compost bucket.

DILLY BEAN RECIPE

4 lbs. green snap beans
5 cups apple cider or white vinegar
5 cups water
¹/₂ cup salt

Pack jars with beans and add:
¹/₄ tsp. cayenne
¹/₂ tsp. whole mustard seed
¹/₂ tsp. dill seed
1 or 2 garlic cloves

Fill jars with brine, secure lids. Process in boiling water bath for 15 minutes.

Procedure:

1. Wash six quart or 12 pint jars. Set out to rinse.
2. Sterilize jars in several inches of boiling water for 10 minutes. Place jars open-side down on a clean, dry towel until ready to fill. It is important to avoid touching the insides or the mouths of the jars once they are sterile.
3. Sterilize dome lids by covering them with boiled water in a bowl or pot.
4. Create the brine in a large pot; mix and bring to a boil:
   - **5 cups apple cider or white vinegar**
   - **5 cups water**
   - **¹/₂ cup salt**
3. Prepare the vegetables to be pickled. Rinse thoroughly. For beans, snap off stems. For cucumbers, cut off blossom and stem ends and quarter lengthwise.
4. Into jars put dill tops, cayenne, mustard, and garlic to taste, or refer to recipe that follows.
5. Pack jars full with prepared beans or cucumbers.
6. Ladle the hot brine over the vegetables, filling the jar to one-half inch from the top. A special canning funnel works well for this operation.
7. Tap jars on the tabletop to release any trapped air bubbles.
8. Place sterilized lids on jars and secure rings.
9. Place full capped jars into a canning pot, making sure water covers the tops of all jars. Bring to a boil for 15 minutes.
10. Using jar grippers, remove processed jars from heat and cover with a cloth. Remove the rings on each jar, making sure the dome lids are sealed. Store in a cool, dry place away from direct light. Pickles are best eaten after they have been put up for at least two weeks.

Important note: If any jar does not seal properly, store in the refrigerator and enjoy over the first week or two. If any stored jars are found without a good seal, contents should be thrown out and composted. Bacteria found in unsealed or unprocessed jars are extremely harmful to your health.

Edible Jewelry
Making Veggie Necklaces

Preschool through grade two groups will need close supervision with this activity.

Purpose: To make wearable art from the harvest.

Discovery Question: What jewelery designs can we create with the food we grow?

Materials: Carrots, peas, green beans, dried fruits (apples, bananas, etc.), thick thread, sharp knives (adults should do the cutting and chopping), cutting board, and very large sewing needle (knitting needles also work well).

Procedure:

1. Adults cut carrots into thin, but sturdy, slices. You may choose to punch out the cores or leave them intact.
2. Shell peas and chop beans into small pieces.
3. Place vegetables in bowls on a table together with dried fruit. Thread a needle for each participant. Tie both ends of the thread or string together in a knot large enough to hold the vegetables on the thread.
4. Create patterned necklaces and bracelets by threading the needle through the veggie pieces one at a time.
5. Discuss the different patterns you have created. Color coordinate. Feel free to eat your works of art.
6. For longer-lasting jewelry, hang to dry in a dark, cool, dry place.

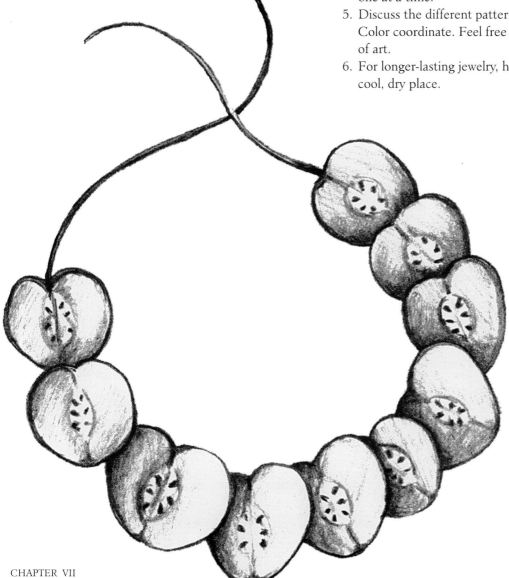

Carrot Cooking Care
Experiment with the Best Way to Prepare Veggies

Purpose: To determine the most nutritious way of preparing vegetables that keeps the vitamins intact.

Discovery Question: What cooking method preserves the most vitamins?

Materials: Carrots, stove, steamer, two pots, and clear glasses.

Procedure:

1. Slice up the carrots.
2. Boil half the carrots. Steam the other half by putting your portable steamer in the bottom of a pot, adding about an inch of water, placing the carrots in the steamer, and bringing to a boil for three to five minutes.
3. When fully cooked, pour the water from the boiled carrots and the steamed carrots into separate clear glasses.
4. Which is darker? The orange-yellow coloring of the water is actually the vitamins that have been boiled out of the carrots. Which contains more vitamins—the boiled carrots or the steamed carrots? How about the raw ones?
   Important note: The deeper orange the water is colored, the fewer vitamins remaining in the vegetables when you eat them.
5. This activity can also be done with spinach or squash.

Presto Pesto!
Making Pesto Pizza

Making pesto pizza is fun, interesting, and tasty. This activity is designed to be started in the fall with the planting of garlic—an essential ingredient to making homemade pesto pizza. The rest of the ingredients can be planted in the spring and harvested during late summer or fall.

Purpose: To research and grow the ingredients for making pesto pizza.

Discovery Question: Can all the ingredients for pesto pizza be grown locally?

Procedure:

1. Local research: Interview parents, community members, local chefs, etc., to collect recipes for pesto.
2. Research which ingredients can be grown locally. Find out when they need to be planted.
3. Choose a pesto recipe, or create your own, utilizing locally grown ingredients.
4. Prepare garden space, and plant garlic in the fall. In warmer climates, garlic can be planted in the spring.
5. Conduct research to obtain information about ingredients that cannot be grown locally: call your agricultural extension office, use an encyclopedia, or check the Internet. Children may also want to research the history of pesto, the history of pizza, the plant ingredients, geography of the areas where these plants are grown, and nutritional information about the pesto ingredients.
6. Call and visit local farms to find out about cheese production for your pizza. Check out the possibility of getting flour from a mill in your area.
7. Procure seeds/seedlings for the ingredients to be grown for pesto recipe.
8. Plant and cultivate the plants for your pesto recipe through the summer.
9. Harvest the ingredients and follow the recipe to make pesto. (You can freeze any excess pesto.)
10. Prepare dough for pizza crust and bake until almost done. Spread pesto on crust and return to oven for several mintues. Eat and enjoy!

SAMPLE PESTO RECIPE

1$\frac{1}{2}$ cups of fresh basil leaves (you may also add spinach, parsley, or cilantro to the basil)
2–5 cloves of garlic, peeled (according to taste)
$\frac{1}{4}$ cup pine nuts
$\frac{1}{4}$ cup freshly grated Parmesan cheese
$\frac{1}{4}$ cup freshly squeezed lemon juice

1. Put the basil, garlic, pine nuts, and Parmesan cheese in a blender or food processor.
2. Turn the machine on and drizzle in the lemon juice.
3. Continue to puree until a smooth paste is formed.

To Freeze Pesto

Make pesto in volume during the summer when fresh basil is plentiful, and freeze it in one-cup quantities for use year-round. Each packet is enough to make a large pizza; or mix it with pasta, tortellini, or ravioli.

Just Chew It
Creating a Vegetable Nutrition Poster and Advertising Campaign

Created by Diana King of Orange, Vermont.

Purpose: To learn about the nutritional value of garden-grown vegetables. To start an advertising campaign promoting fresh vegetables.

Discovery Question: What is the nutritional content of the fresh vegetables growing in our garden? How can we let others in our school and community know about the nutritional value of fresh vegetables?

Materials: Vegetable nutrition chart, a variety of poster materials, and popular advertisements from magazines and newspapers.

Procedure:

1. As a group, discuss the value of eating vegetables, the vitamin content of various vegetables, and what each of these vitamins does for our bodies.

2. Look at examples of popular advertisements in magazines and newspapers. Discuss the strengths and weaknesses of each ad. What product is being promoted? What message is being conveyed along with the product? What is the connection between the product and the message?

3. The group breaks into different teams with each team assigned a vegetable. The teams must develop posters promoting the health benefits of their assigned vegetable. Each poster must include:
   a) At least three reasons why the vegetable is good for you.
   b) A large picture of the vegetable that is easy to identify.
   c) A description of the look, taste, smell, feel, and sound of the vegetable.

4. Have a poster contest, assigning awards for the most creative, the most descriptive, the clearest message, etc.

5. Place these posters around the community to promote the sale of your garden vegetables.

Extensions:

1. Children create their own video advertisements for various vegetables. Write scripts, create sets and props, edit, and add music to the video. This is especially fun when the ads are spoofs of actual TV commercials.

2. Contact your local cable-access channel and have these homemade ads run on the air. Use their equipment to make the ads, if possible.

3. Hold a contest to see which vegetable can inspire the most creative advertising campaign. Run the ads on local TV with a phone number listed for viewers to call in and vote. The winning team receives a free crate of their vegetable.

4. Vegetable soap operas: Students write scripts depicting the trials and tribulations of vegetables growing in the garden. For instance: The orphan tomato plant who grew up next to a bunch of sunlight-greedy sunflowers and was withering badly, but was discovered by a local talent scout and transplanted to a nearby row of onions where it thrived; or the story of the potato patch that was invaded by voracious potato beetles until their leaves were sprayed by organic pest spray and they were saved. Cross pollinate ideas.

Everybody Freeze!
Blanching, Bagging, and Freezing Fresh Vegetables

Purpose: To learn the proper techniques for blanching and freezing fresh vegetables

Discovery Questions: How can we save the fresh foods we have in our garden for the winter?

Materials: Steamer pot, water, stop watch, stove top, desired vegetables: asparagus, beans, broccoli, corn, etc.

Procedure:

1. Fill the steamer pot with an inch or two of water and heat to boiling.
2. Prepare vegetables: cut broccoli into spears, shear corn from the cob, remove the ends of beans, etc.
3. Put prepared vegetables into a steamer basket, and place in the steamer pot after the water comes to a boil. Allow to steam for three minutes, and remove immediately. This process is called blanching.
4. Quickly place vegetables into a bowl of ice water and allow to sit momentarily.
5. Place vegetables in a strainer. Allow them to drain briefly in order to remove excess water, then place the vegetables in freezer bags or plastic containers (yogurt containers or Tupperware work well).
6. Label and place in the freezer as quickly as possible. Speed is the key to quality in this process.

Popular Vegetables
with blanching times
of exactly three minutes

Asparagus

Green Beans

Broccoli*

Cauliflower

Corn

Collard Greens

Swiss Chard

Mustard Greens

Beet Greens

Spinach

*soak in salt water for a half hour
before blanching to remove worms

What's Cookin'
Making a Youth Garden Harvest Cookbook

Purpose: To create a community cookbook, consisting of recipes using vegetables and herbs from the youth garden and from ingredients traditionally grown in gardens in the community.

Discovery Question: How can we collect and compile recipes using garden-grown vegetables and herbs?

Materials: Art supplies for making a homemade cookbook: construction paper, scissors, crayons, paints, hole punch, string or thread, and glue.

Procedure:

1. Collect recipes for every dish that you created with garden-grown vegetables this summer. Include a range of dishes from very simple, like cucumber sandwiches, to gourmet, like pesto pizza.
2. Brainstorm for improvements on these recipes. Include substitutions.
3. Create and test your own recipes, using garden ingredients. Check the Specialty Food Product activity on page 52.
4. Interview a parent, relative, neighbor, and/or local chef to get their favorite garden recipes.
5. Decide on a sensible format for the cookbook.
6. Organize the recipes into chapters by category: salads, desserts, etc.
7. Brainstorm a number of special features to make this local cookbook unique: photographs and quotations of community members; illustrations— drawings and diagrams; stories, poems, and songs; traditions and memories connected to the recipes; anecdotes from the youth garden; a preface by a well-known local personality.
8. Choose a title. A group of artists can make an eye-catching title page.
9. Solicit donations to pay for printing. Conduct a raffle or silent auction. Ask a local business to co-sponsor the cookbook, sell advertising space.
10. Sell the cookbook to raise money for gardening supplies next year.

You're Grounded
Putting the Garden to Bed

Purpose: To prepare the garden for winter in a way that will minimize weeds and maximize soil fertility for the spring.

Discovery Question: What do we need to do to prepare our garden for winter and for planting next spring? Why is it important to clean up the garden before winter?

Materials: Standard garden tools.

Procedure:

1. **Clean out all the beds.** After the garden is completely harvested, each of the beds must be thoroughly cleared of all weeds and plant parts from the annual crops that had been growing there. This includes all leaves, stems, and roots. Perennial flowers and herbs should not be removed and should be allowed to die naturally. Use the plant parts removed from the garden to build a compost pile. Do not, however, use any diseased or insect-infested material in the compost. Dispose of these elsewhere.

2. **Conduct a soil test, and add appropriate soil amendments.** An end-of-season soil test is useful for determining what amendments you should add to your soil, and how much. For information on how to conduct a soil test, see page 38. Soil amendments frequently added in the fall include lime, rock powders, green sand, and rotted hay and manures.

3. **Plant spring bulbs.** Fall is the time to plant spring flowers such as tulips, daffodils, crocuses, lilies, and peonies. Plant on or close to the first frost date for your region, up until the ground freezes. For northern gardeners, garlic should be planted in the fall for a summer harvest.

4. **Cover crop.** The areas where annual flowers and vegetables are to be planted in the spring can be cover cropped; that is, seeded with a fast-growing plant such as buckwheat, oats, annual rye, and certain clovers. Turn it over in early spring to create a "green manure."

5. **Tool maintenance.** Clean your tools. To protect from rust, oil them lightly, and store in a dry place.

Mix Well for Best Results
Community Harvest Celebration

Purpose: To share the harvest with the whole community, and to celebrate the children's accomplishments in the youth garden.

Discovery Question: How can we include the larger community in our harvesttime activities?

Materials: A season's worth of harvested crops, invitations, crafts from summer activities, storytellers, dancers, musicians, etc.

Procedure:

1. Choose a date and rain date (very important) for the harvest festival. Borrow chairs, tables, and utensils from a school, church, or senior center.
2. Have the children design invitations and posters using the garden's logo, and distribute to family, friends, and businesses that donated goods and services, as well as farmers who came to lecture, the local media, etc.
3. Have children sign up to bring a potluck dish (appetizer, entree, salad, and dessert) using as many garden-grown ingredients as possible. If you have access to a kitchen during the program, prepare make-ahead dishes, like casseroles that can be frozen, preserves, pickles, dried fruits, and vegetables.
4. Decorate with dried flowers, corn stalks, autumn leaves, photos, and artwork the children made during the program; make centerpieces for the tables from garden produce.
5. On the day of the celebration, have participants and guests finish up harvesting and preparing the garden for winter.
6. Have craftspeople work with produce to make holiday harvest gifts.
7. Arrange a program of music, stories, and dance. Schedule a time for the children to share experiences, read stories and poems about the garden, and a time for parents to share their appreciation.
8. Sell copies of the garden cookbook to raise money for next year's program.
9. Eat, drink, and be merry!

Young actors ham it up at this Harvest Celebration.

The Food Works
Harvest Celebration Recipe

Ingredients:

- ✔ a garden with crops to be harvested
- ✔ willing hands
- ✔ fresh-pressed cider
- ✔ invitations
- ✔ rain date
- ✔ access to a kitchen for food preparation
- ✔ a community-wide harvest potluck
- ✔ tables and chairs
- ✔ music, fiddler, songs
- ✔ storyteller
- ✔ dancing
- ✔ craftspeople
- ✔ paintings, stories, and crafts that children created over the season
- ✔ baskets to collect harvest
- ✔ gardening tools
- ✔ press release
- ✔ local media, if you want
- ✔ camera
- ✔ children to share their experiences
- ✔ parents to share their appreciation
- ✔ elders

Mix well for best results. Serves a community.

Life Lab's Growing Community of Learners

– by Lisa Glick, Education & Outreach Director, Life Lab Science Program

Gardens are powerful learning tools. School gardens put the natural world at a student's fingertips, and provide a rich context for investigating the world we live in. As educators, we continually have the opportunity to nurture each child's curiosity and desire to explore. Whether in a planter box, an outdoor garden, or an indoor growing area, gardens can enhance the study of science, nutrition, social studies, math, language arts, and much more.

Many discoveries take place in a garden setting: a spider spinning its web, the realization that spinach tastes good, the awareness that a soil ecosystem contains living organisms. Historically, the importance of school gardens has long been recognized. In 1910, there were 81,000 school gardens in Europe, and major projects flowering in Massachusetts, Ohio, and New York. In 1911, Dora Williams noted in her book, *Gardens and Their Meanings,* that "A school garden worth the name is not a teacher's garden, or a philanthropist's garden, but a garden worked out in thought and act by happy, purposeful children."

At Life Lab we have been supporting garden-based learning since 1979, when students and teachers developed a small garden at Green Acres Elementary School in Santa Cruz, California. Teachers there soon discovered their students engaged in science inquiries through gardening, and enjoying it thoroughly. The idea grew rapidly, attracting attention from other school districts, parents, universities, and community leaders. Since that very first school garden was developed as a living laboratory, Life Lab has facilitated the use of gardens as outdoor classroom learning environments through dynamic professional development and implementation of effective curriculum materials in over 1,000 schools, ranging from California to Ohio and Alaska to Florida.

As educators we have the responsibility to prepare children for the world of tomorrow. Although we can't see that world, we can challenge students to ask questions, to develop processes for thinking, and to search for answers, as well as to communicate, work, and live cooperatively. In collaboration with the University of California, Santa Cruz and its award-winning Center

for Agroecology and Sustainable Food Systems, we are establishing Life Lab's Growing Classroom model school garden learning center. This facility will be a unique educational resource for professional development supporting integrated teaching through garden-based education, as well as specially designed interactive programs for children, families, and UCSC students.

As we move forward into the 21st century, we encourage you to join us in the exciting and important work of creating school gardens as outdoor classrooms.

8

Harvesting the Results:
Evaluation and Assessment Tool Kit

Crucial to the long-term success of any youth gardening program is implementing a system for monitoring the effectiveness of the horticultural practices, nutritional exercises, community-service experiences, and all other educational activities over the course of the project. Assessment and evaluation are vital to the survival of any program. It is through these processes that the value and success of the program can be demonstrated, and the quality of the activities can be sustained and improved.

The design and implementation of a purposeful assessment and evaluation plan obviously require additional time and effort. Ultimately, the short- and long-term benefits gained by the leaders, the students, and the program as a result of this effort make that time well worth the investment. In the following sections of this chapter, the purpose of assessment and evaluation is discussed, along with the differences between the two and the benefits both provide. A bread-making activity is given as one example of using a gardening lesson as two activities (instruction and assessment) in one. Next, we discuss the tools for starting and using an assessment portfolio—to aid in the process of assessing and evaluating the overall garden program. Based on the assessments made over the course of the project, an authoritative and well-documented evaluation can be completed using the forms at the end of the chapter.

Why Assess?

In so many walks of life, administrators and educators must justify their work with concrete data and results that show the effectiveness of their program. Without reliable statistics and evidence, they are left with only anecdotal evidence that can be limited and doesn't carry sufficient weight for policy makers.

A rigorous assessment procedure is particularly useful for ongoing supporters of children's gardens. If the organizers can document precisely how they have met the needs outlined in the program's mission, they will have a powerful local model to encourage advocates and funders to continue their support and provide incentive for new backers to come on board.

The core reason for conducting ongoing assessments, however, should never be forgotten: to offer communities practical, proven methods for implementing an ecological education program that has a lasting effect on the lives of children. With these results in hand, leaders have the perfect entree for demonstrating to teachers, school boards, administrators, and community members why their gardening program should become a major focus for every school curriculum. This is a bridge, a rationale for why and how children learn through gardening, and why it is essential to connect gardens to the lives of schools.

Assessing and evaluating the value of an entire program is no simple task. For the experienced or novice garden educator, the task of organizing, planning, and conducting a garden program to meet the diversity of youth interests—not to mention maintaining a successful garden—is itself an ambitious undertaking. What is often overlooked amid all the details is the critical need for ongoing documentation in order to assess every step of the process.

If the documentation tools are put into place from the beginning, however, then the assessment and evaluation methods will be integrated in the program on an ongoing basis. For example, the garden educator can use creative arts activities to teach nutrition and horticulture lessons, collecting samples of students' artwork as well as recording their verbal reactions to specific food activities in the garden journal. Both the artwork and the oral responses are forms of documentation that can be used to assess and evaluate the program.

Quantitative assessment should not become an obsession, but rather one piece in a sustainable program. While it may seem self-evident that gardening works to feed the whole child, anecdotal observation alone is not enough to convince the wider community of its effectiveness. Potential supporters and the general public will need a combination of stories, samples of student work, produce and products, newspaper clippings, and a variety of detailed visual documentation such as photographs and video, combined with more quantitative evaluation evidence, all described in greater detail below.

The Assessment/ Evaluation Process

Assessment and evaluation are not the same, yet the words are often used interchangeably. Unfortunately, so are the concept and practice of the two. Assessment is a *qualitative monitoring of process*. Evaluation is a *quantitative categorizing of product*. Assessment assists students or programs in meeting specific criteria—i.e., learning specific knowledge, skills, and attitudes. These ongoing assessments prepare students to succeed when it comes time for final evaluation in those areas.

The Assessment Process

Assessment involves monitoring and gathering information about a program's progress over time. It is an ongoing process. **Evaluation** entails placing a value on a specific project, product, or performance once completed. An evaluation is based on the assessments made and recorded over the course of the program.

Assessment is intended to provide an opportunity to monitor how well the student or program is progressing toward specific expectations or outcomes. Assessment should be informative, direct instruction or implementation, and ultimately prepares a student or program for success at the final evaluation. Assess-

Telling Your Story

The distinctiveness of your site in your unique bioregion and the relationships that are formed—between children, elders, the community, and with the garden itself—create the text for a very moving and meaningful story. Sharing this story through photos, slides, and anecdotes can generate interest about the ability of a garden to motivate children, change behavior, teach lifelong lessons, and build a caring community.

But telling the story of your children's garden has an importance that goes far beyond demonstrating its effectiveness in a report or press release. The story has its own magic and its own life. It creates a living roadmap of your project's journey, generating its own energy that stirs imaginations and nurtures new relationships. It

inspires new ways of thinking, transforming the world in ways unimaginable before the story began.

The story celebrates the uniqueness of every place. It transcends the data and statistics to establish a sense of place and of purpose. Garden stories foster appreciation and understanding of a community and of one another, emanating from the vibrations of the land itself, shaping the lives of people to create something new—something uniquely their own.

A story is a powerful testament about who we are, why we are here, what we are part of, and where we belong. It is part of the larger history of how people have struggled to learn how to live with one another. A story is part of a continuous trail of remembering the ancient wisdom that blooms in

each new generation, and unfolds as a community comes together to nurture food and children.

Gardening is also about rediscovering the story of your community's agricultural heritage. Whether you are in an urban, rural, or suburban setting, the land you live on was almost certainly an area where people once lived and grew their own food. By including elders in this process, you can begin to tap into the traditional knowledge, folklore, skills, and stories of your community that have been passed down over time. They can provide the initial link, the key that opens the doors to the stories, practices, techniques, and foods that have been used in your home. It is this connection between past and future that the garden story enlivens.

ment is not an end in itself, but rather a means of achieving that end.

The three basic forms of assessment are: activities, tasks, and tools (scoring guides). These assessments are used differently, yet all serve the same purpose of helping to gather information on a student's or program's progress.

1. An assessment is any classroom lesson or activity which engages students in a way that allows the teacher to be both instructing and assessing at the same time. A sample of how an activity becomes an assessment activity is described below.

2. Assessment tasks are informal measures that are deliberately designed to "check in" to see how well students are progressing. Typical assessment tasks include journal writing, conferencing, creating graphic organizers such as Venn diagrams and concept webs, and taking opinion surveys.

3. Assessment tools (scoring guides) are formal measures against which a student's or program's progress is compared. Rubrics and checklists are two standard assessment tools. In both cases, specific criteria (expected outcomes/indicators of success) are listed along with a continuum that reflects where the student or program stands in terms of progress toward those expected outcomes.

The Evaluation Process

Evaluation is assigning value to a final product or performance. Unlike assessment, evaluation is a quantitative process. Typically, a product or performance is given a grade, a percentage, or some other numerical designation that reflects the number of pre-determined criteria the product or performance has met.

Evaluation can be more objective than assessment. The criteria for evaluation are clearly stated

A Word about Patience

Clearly, the goal is for a summer garden to grow into a curriculum for the local school as a source of lifelong learning. But as any gardener and farmer well knows, it takes all of the right conditions—nutrient-rich soil, proper rainfall, enough warmth and sunlight, as well as the mindful human touch at precisely the right moments, plus a smidgen of magic—to insure a bountiful yield. It is rare indeed for these conditions to synchronize in one growing season the first time around.

At Food Works, we have found that it is vital to maintain a consistent and clear vision for how to promote the garden as a year-round learning experience for all members of a community. Still, with a strong vision and all the available resources, it can take years to build the bridge from the summer garden to the year-round school curriculum. Each garden takes on a life of its own, a unique personality that is impossible to predict.

Try to avoid unrealistic expectations that can cause unnecessary frustrations. Not every garden can grow into a curriculum, but every garden can touch the lives of all who are involved in its growth.

beforehand and extensively taught, reinforced, and assessed. Continuous assessment informs students of their progress in those particular areas, and informs teachers how to better assist students in meeting their goals. Ongoing assessment prepares students to succeed at the time of final evaluation. Unlike assessment, evaluation is an end in itself.

Assessing and Evaluating a Program Goal

One of the goals of teaching nutrition through food growing is to encourage children to develop a healthy respect and appreciation for food and balanced nutrition. Having established this goal, the educator is now able to deliberately plan a series of activities that will enable students to achieve it. One of those activities might be bread making (see sample activity below).

Keeping a clear goal in mind also allows the teacher to plan what assessment tasks and tools will be used so that the teacher and students can monitor how well they are progressing toward meeting this goal. Tasks will include pre-, mid- and post-assessments that might involve affective surveys (measuring students' attitudes), journal writing, meal logs (daily records of what they're eating), and concept webs (measuring students' acquisition of knowledge—in this case, knowledge about nutrition). Tools will include the more formal rubrics or checklists the teacher has designed. These periodic assessments not only monitor progress and direct instruction, but also reinforce the knowledge, skills, and attitudes students are developing.

When students are given many opportunities through various assessment activities, tasks, and tools to develop the knowledge, skills, and attitudes expected of them, they are prepared to be evaluated in those areas.

One example of an evaluation related to the goal of understanding nutrition could be for the data in students' meal logs to be compared to a food pyramid and converted to actual food-group choice percentages that would serve as the final evaluation. This final evaluation *objectively quantifies a performance* (i.e., how well did our daily eating patterns match food pyramid requirements?) that demonstrates whether or not students have met the specific criteria that were the focus of instruction and assessment.

Bread Making: A Sample Lesson Integrating Assessment and Instruction

Instructing students on the nutritional value of bread, then allowing them to make, bake, and eat their own bread, aligns directly with the goal of encouraging balanced nutrition. National research has shown that children demonstrate a much greater appreciation for food that they have helped cultivate and prepare than food that has been provided by someone else.

Bread making can easily become an assessment activity, allowing the teacher to instruct and assess at the same time.

For example, before beginning the lesson, the teacher can first conduct a pre-assessment that gauges students' knowledge and attitudes about bread and nutrition. This task might take the form of a survey asking students to describe what they think or feel about bread. A journal entry about how many times and in how many different forms they have eaten bread in the last week could serve as both a knowledge and attitude pre-assessment. A third possibility is to ask students to draw a picture showing how bread is made. These pre-assessments will reveal much about students' experience and attitudes and help direct instruction.

Once the pre-assessments are completed, students can begin learning about the nutritional value of bread and how bread is made. During instruction and class discussion, ongoing assessment can be made by noting observations of certain students and directing questions back to points made in the pre-assessments.

After providing students with necessary background information (some of which may be determined by the results of pre-assessments), students can begin to make, bake, and eat their own bread. As they are participating in this process, the teacher can again listen to their conversations, observe their behaviors and levels of participation, and record these observations in an assessment portfolio. A "mid-assessment" can also be conducted to assess whether students' initial attitudes about bread are changing now that they are more personally involved in the bread making process.

After the students bake and eat their own bread, it's time for a post-assessment. For a direct before and after comparison, students can be given the same task as they were given for the pre-assessment activities. Any one of the three pre-assessments described earlier would be excellent for comparing before and after pictures of the students' knowledge and attitudes.

Another way to incorporate assessment into activities is to design activities that are actual assessments themselves. Problem-solving activities in which students must apply knowledge and skills they've learned are excellent ways to instruct and assess at the same time.

For example, once students have received instruction in the ingredients and nutritional value of bread, pass out several different bread mixes with varying proportions of ingredients. Students are then asked to rank each mix according to nutritional value, predict which will come out as "bread as we know it," realign the mixes to their correct proportions, or even attempt to create their own "special mix." Through these activities, students can learn additional information about the process of bread making, and the leader can assess what they know based on how they apply their knowledge toward solving these problems.

Assessment tells us how well we're doing, what is working, what is not, and where to go next. If we assess as we go, not only are we able to increase the amount of information we obtain about our students, but also we are able to monitor the effectiveness of

A parent volunteer helps children bake their own bread in a school's homemade outdoor bread oven. This activity alone fosters skills and knowledge in math, science, nutrition, and history.

individual activities as well as the design of the program. Leaders and students are more informed, instruction improves, and the effectiveness and success of the overall program are enhanced.

Garden Program Assessment Criteria

Important note: Video recording is a great way to document product and performance.

🌱 *Student Assessments/Evaluations* — a dated collection of student assessment activities, tasks, tools, and student evaluations.

🌱 *Student Products and Performances* — a collection of dated student work that documents development of knowledge, skills, attitudes, and attainment of program goals.

🌱 *Student Affective Surveys* — a collection of dated surveys that students periodically fill out, expressing their opinions, feelings, and attitudes about the program and activities.

🌱 *Anecdotal Observations/Reflections* — a diary that chronicles the success of the program through periodic reflections from the teacher.

🌱 *Participation/Attendance Graphs* — daily records of student and community-member attendance and participation that can later be analyzed for trends.

🌱 *Community Impact Scrapbook* — a collection of fliers, newspaper articles, photographs, quotations, etc., that document the program's impact on the community.

🌱 *Culminating Activity Surveys* — a collection of surveys completed by participants (parents, community members, school officials) attending the various culminating activities. Culminating activities might include tours of the gardens, student-produced community meals, final harvests for local food banks, Open Houses, Final Project exhibits, Garden Fair projects, and any other activities that allow students to demonstrate the skills and knowledge they have acquired, based on the garden-program goals.

Assessing and Evaluating the Overall Garden Program

Here the broader task of how to assess and evaluate an overall garden program is outlined.

A highly effective method for monitoring and assessing a garden program involves developing and maintaining an ongoing assessment portfolio. A portfolio is a collection of products, performances, assessments, and other evidence documenting a program through the course of its implementation. A portfolio tells the garden's story.

Here is a list of steps to be taken to assess the effectiveness of a garden program using an assessment portfolio:

1. Determine the overall goals of the garden unit, being as specific as possible.

2. In the program plan, design activities and exercises that will help children meet those goals.

3. Through the course of the season, implement assessment activities, tasks, and tools that reflect the content and goals of the program (see "Assessment Criteria" below).

4. Collect these activities, tasks, and tools as you go, and include them in an Assessment Portfolio. By the end of the program, this Assessment Portfolio should contain multiple examples of each of the criteria listed below, telling a detailed story of the effectiveness of the program.

A garden program Assessment Portfolio can include, but is not limited to, the criteria listed on the previous page.

Garden Program Evaluation

Ideally, throughout the course of the garden program, participants are provided with multiple opportunities to explore the areas in which they are to be evaluated. By collecting information and monitoring the other indicators of success listed under "Assessment Criteria," the entire garden program will have that same opportunity for success in its final evaluation.

Below are examples of ways to evaluate the Assessment Criteria for a garden program. A check in every box indicates a very successful program.

❏ Student affective surveys reflect a greater percentage of positive remarks than negative remarks.

❏ Anecdotal observations/reflections by the teacher are more positive than negative.

❏ Participation/attendance graphs indicate an increase in participation.

❏ Community impact scrapbook reflects positive public relations and steady or increasing exposure.

❏ Student assessments/evaluations show a progression in knowledge and skills.

❏ Student products/performances demonstrate a proficiency in skills and knowledge application.

❏ Culminating activity evaluations generally reflect positive responses

Assessment and Evaluation Forms

The following forms are ready-to-use tools for conducting ongoing assessments and a final evaluation of a garden program linked directly to the program's goals. The *Ongoing Garden Program Accountability Log* is for documenting information about week-by-week learning activities. This can help determine the reasons for success (or lack of success) at the conclusion of the program.

The *Garden Program Effectiveness Sheet* contains questions for creating a narrative summary of the program's effectiveness incorporating the activities, assessments, and evaluation offered through the course of the season.

The final two sheets pertain to the growth and success of the garden itself, The *Garden Seed-to-Harvest Data Sheet*, and the *Garden Site Improvement Plan*. The *Seed-to-Harvest Data Sheet* is particularly important to have on hand throughout the course of the growing season to keep track of the care and maintenance of the garden—a crucial indicator of the program's success.

Program Portfolio Cover Sheet

This is a record-keeping form to track assessments throughout the course of the program. Each time an assessment in any of the categories is placed in the portfolio, mark the date it was entered. A good balance of documentation, featuring many examples of each of these assessment types, will provide a more complete, holistic picture of your program. At the conclusion of the program, an Exemplar Program Portfolio can be created, including the best pieces from each assessment category.

1. **Student Assessments/Evaluations** — student assessment activities, tasks and tools, and evaluations (tests, quizzes, etc.).
2. **Student Products and Performances** — student work that traces the development of knowledge, skills, and attitudes and documents the attainment of program goals.
3. **Student Affective Surveys** — surveys that students periodically fill out expressing their opinions, feelings, and attitudes about the program and activities.
4. **Anecdotal Observations/Reflections** — a diary chronicling the success of the program through periodic reflections from the teacher.
5. **Participation/Attendance Graphs** — daily records of student and community member attendance and participation that can later be analyzed for trends.

6. **Community Impact Scrapbook** — fliers, newspaper articles, photographs, quotations, etc., documenting the program's impact on the community.
7. **Culminating Activity Surveys** — surveys completed by participants (e.g., parents, community members, school officials) attending the program's various culminating activities. Culminating activities might include tours of the gardens, community meals, harvests for local food banks, Open Houses, Final Project exhibits, Garden Fair projects, and any other activities demonstrating skill and knowledge that students have acquired according to the criteria by which the program is evaluated.

Important note: For some of the above, video recording can document the product or performance and also capture affective evidence, which might otherwise be difficult to document.

1) STUDENT ASSESSMENTS/ EVALUATIONS	2) STUDENT PRODUCTS/ PERFORMANCES	3) STUDENT AFFECTIVE SURVEYS	4) ANECDOTAL OBSERVATIONS/ REFLECTIONS	5) PARTICIPATION/ ATTENDANCE GRAPHS	6) COMMUNITY IMPACT SCRAPBOOKS	7) CULMINATING ACTIVITY SURVEYS

Student Portfolio Cover Sheet

Similar to the Program Portfolio, the Student Portfolio contains all the assessments that the student creates or is given throughout the program. This Student Portfolio is kept by the teacher, but is accessible to students anytime, enabling them to monitor their progress in meeting the goals of the program on an ongoing basis. As with the Program Portfolio Cover Sheet, each time an assessment product in any of the categories is placed in the portfolio, mark the date it was entered. At the conclusion of the program, an Exemplar Student Portfolio can be created using the best pieces from each assessment category. These Exemplar Portfolios are particularly valuable in evaluating the gardening program at its conclusion.

1. ***Student Assessments/Evaluations*** — student assessment activities, tasks and tools, and evaluations (tests, quizzes, etc.).

2. ***Student Products and Performances*** — student work that traces the development of knowledge, skills, and attitudes, and documents the attainment of program goals. This includes the student's culminating activity.

3. ***Student Affective Surveys*** — surveys that the student periodically fills out expressing his or her opinions, feelings, and attitudes about the program and activities.

4. ***Anecdotal Observations/Reflections*** — a diary chronicling the student's progress through periodic reflections from the teacher.

1) STUDENT ASSESSMENTS/ EVALUATIONS	2) STUDENT PRODUCTS/ PERFORMANCES	3) STUDENT AFFECTIVE SURVEYS	4) ANECDOTAL OBSERVATIONS/ REFLECTIONS

Final Program Evaluation Checklist

This is one example of an evaluation that directly corresponds to the assessment criteria listed on the Program Portfolio Cover Sheet. If the identified assessments are administered on a regular basis in concordance with the program's learning goals, then the final program evaluation can be determined in a very straightforward manner using the checklist below. In this example, a check in every box indicates a successful program.

❑ Student assessments/evaluations show progress in knowledge and skills.

❑ Student products/performances demonstrate a general proficiency in skills and knowledge application.

❑ Culminating activity evaluations have positive responses.

❑ Student affective surveys contain a higher percentage of positive than negative remarks.

❑ The leaders' anecdotal observations/reflections are more positive than negative.

❑ Participation/attendance graphs of students and community members indicate an overall increase in participation.

❑ Community impact scrapbook contains many examples of positive public relations, and steady or increasing exposure.

Garden Program Effectiveness Sheet

The following questions help leaders and participants create a narrative summary of the assessment information collected through the course of the program and evaluated at the program's conclusion. After the evaluation is completed using the Final Program Evaluation Checklist, answering the following questions on a separate sheet will provide a written summary of the program's effectiveness. The Program Portfolio will be strong evidence documenting the conclusions reached below.

Focus Question: Utilizing all of the assessment and evaluation data, how well did you meet the goals and objectives of the program? You may respond in the following key areas:

a. Describe how the program met a diversity of youth interests: educational, horticultural, recreational, social, nutritional, artistic, etc. Be sure to be specific by drawing from the Program Portfolio and exemplar Student Portfolios.

b. How effective was the program in involving the community: including parents and elders, press and media for storytelling, meals and celebrations, arts and theater, food donations, etc.?

c. Describe the benefits and disadvantages of the garden site. For example, did the theme gardens continue to pique the interest of participants? Was there sufficient room for participants and commu-

nity members to share stories, meals, and crafts? Were there effective ongoing communications— i.e., bulletin board, newsletter, etc.?

d. What impact did the garden program have on the self-esteem of the participants? How did growing, preparing, and cooking their own food affect students' diet and nutritional awareness? How did working with elders and other community members influence their attitudes and behavior?

e. How did the program respond to the unpredictable variables inherent in any youth gardening effort?

f. What unexpected surprises arose? Some examples would include an inspired sense of pride in the community, a new culinary delight, a weekly storytelling circle, an improvisational garden theater troupe, a weekly gift to a local food shelf, or a Saturday garden market.

Weekly Garden Program Accountability Log

The purpose of this form is to collect data in a systematic way to analyze factors that contributed to the success of the program. This is not an assessment or evaluation in itself, but rather a data-collection process. After the program evaluation is completed, this information can help determine why particular areas of the program were or were not successful. The information requested should be collected daily, with a separate log sheet created each week of the program. This form can be adapted to meet the particular characteristics of each program.

Name

Location *(watershed)*

Week of: Weekly Theme:

	MON	TUES	WED	THURS	FRI	SAT/SUN	TOTALS
Participation							
Number of students							
Number of community participants							
Guest speakers							
Activities							
Horticulture							
Creative Arts/Theater							
Field Trips							
Nutrition—*food eaten from garden*							
Nutrition—*meals and snacks prepared*							
Outreach							
Community-service activities							
Entrepreneurial activities							
Weather							
Noonday Temperature							
Conditions							

Average number of participants per day:

Percentage of participants returning from previous week:

Recommendations for next week:

End of Year Garden Program Accountability Log

This is a summary of the daily information collected using the Ongoing Garden Program Accountability Log on the previous page. A compilation of this data will provide a clear picture of total participation, the weather, the program activities, community involvement, etc. This is essentially a diagnostic tool to assist in determining the reasons behind success (or shortcomings) of the program.

Name

Location *(watershed)*

PROGRAM TOTALS

Total Participation

Number of students

Number of community participants

Guest speakers

Total Activities

Horticulture

Creative Arts/Theater

Field Trips

Nutrition—*food eaten from the garden*

Nutrition—*meals and snacks prepared*

Recreation

Total Outreach

Community-service activities

Entrepreneurial activities

Average number of participants per day

Weather Notes   *Describe the weather you experienced over the course of the garden program*

Garden Seed-to-Harvest
Data Sheet

This form is for summarizing the growth and development of the garden. The information recorded here is particularly useful for making planning improvements in garden productivity for succeeding years.
(See Garden Site Improvement Plan on the following page.)

Name

Location *(watershed)*

Description and size of community

SEED VARIETIES (HEIRLOOM?)	DATE SEEDED OR TRANSPLANTED	GERMINATION RATE	HARVEST DATE	HARVEST AMOUNT	DESTINATION

Answer the following on the reverse side.

1. Approximate size of garden(s) (in square feet).

2. Description (raised-bed theme gardens, flat with straight rows, etc.).

3. Describe soil type: sandy, clay, silt, loam (or a combination).

4. Planting strategies: monoculture, polyculture, interplanting.

5. Garden characteristics. Describe the following:
   • Compost system.
   • Insect pests and ecological remedies applied.
   • Mulching (grass clippings, leaves, living mulch).
   • Beneficial habitats: birdhouses/feeders. List plants that attracted beneficial insects.

6. Cover crops used.

7. Unique problems: vandalism, lack of rainfall, excess weed growth, ineffective participation.

8. Unique successes: bumper bean crop, volunteer crops, food donations.

Garden Site Improvement Plan

Based on your experience of running a summer gardening program, what changes and modifications would you make to improve your garden site? Remember: the best gardens have an underlying structure (permanent walkways and major beds defined, etc.). Use the reverse side to record your improvement plans.

Access: Was your garden fully accessible to all those who wanted to use it?

Circulation/Walkways: Did your walkways allow all participants to move easily from one garden area to another? Were they wide enough? Were they built to last permanently, with landscape fabric, bark mulch, etc.?

Seating: Was there adequate and inviting multi-use, intergenerational seating?

Growing areas: What was your crop success rate? What grew well? What didn't? What would you do differently next year? Was the garden designed to produce a plentiful and continuous harvest (see Chapter Three)? Were there enough learning activities and stations in each garden to keep children interested throughout the growing season? Was there enough diversity of garden themes and crops to keep participants engaged throughout the summer?

Soil care: What changes took place in your soil over the growing season? Did it dry out? harden up? become heavy? moldy? Did you cover crop? Do you plan to soil test and, if necessary, use additional compost and manure next year?

Beneficial Habitats:
Birds—What kinds of birdbaths, birdhouses, or plantings did you install to attract and maintain a permanent home for insect-eating birds? What improvements might be in order for next season?
Pests— How did you respond to pest problems and diseases in the garden (insects, squirrels, skunks, plant diseases, etc.)? Were any perennial beneficial habitat areas specifically designed and cultivated?

Sunlight: Did the garden site receive enough sun to grow a diversity of crops successfully? Were there enough shade devices and strategies (multi-story planting) to prevent early bolting and wilting?

Water: Was the amount of rainfall your garden site received over the season adequate? Was your watering/irrigation system effective for deep watering of the crops? How would you correct any watering problems you experienced at your site?

Compost: Did you have a well designed, well-maintained, and effective compost system (i.e., triple-bin, two-week turnaround, or compost tumbler)?

Weeding/Mulching: Was the garden weeded regularly? What kinds of mulches, if any, did you use (grass clippings, etc., or a living mulch such as Dutch White Clover)?

Safety: Were there any accidents in the garden? What changes could be made in the garden to minimize the chance of personal injury?

Security: Were there any problems with vandalism in the garden? Did the garden have any fences, gates, or locks? Was there regular adult supervision of the garden?

Bulletin Board: Did you have a garden bulletin board and communication exchange area?

Central Meeting Area: Was there a central meeting space in the garden for classes, workshops, creative arts, and food and nutrition activities?

Tool Care and Storage: Did you have regular access to garden tools, watering cans, wheelbarrows, etc.? Where did you store them?

Improvements: What are the estimated costs of proposed improvements? Develop a multi-year timeline for implementation.

The Compassionate Report Card: Caring for Nature and Ourselves at the Edible Schoolyard

– by David Hawkins, Garden Manager of the Edible Schoolyard, Berkeley, California

One of the unfortunate effects of a competitive educational system based on grades is that many students already feel like failures before they even arrive in middle school. For them the classroom has become an arena for daily humiliation, no matter how able and well intentioned the teacher. In our Edible Schoolyard at Martin Luther King, Jr. Middle School in Berkeley, California, we are finding that this pressure often can be left behind when the students come to work in the garden.

At the Edible Schoolyard, students who may not be succeeding in class can attain a degree of success and pride in their individual and collective achievement. The garden's emergence on a derelict weed patch is a source of pride and hope to many of the 500 sixth and seventh graders at King who have created it. Our hope is that the cooperation that exists in the garden will inspire more cooperative approaches to learning in the classroom.

At the end of a class held in the garden, we usually gather in the straw-bale circle and talk about the day's experience. I thank the students for their work, and I remind them to look at what changes they have brought about during the class. One day in the circle a boy said, "Mr. Hawkins, you thanked us for working, but I really didn't work hard."

I thought for a moment. It was a fair comment.

"I was watching you, and what you say is true," I told him. "In fact, you did almost nothing."

A few students snickered.

"There may be a lot of reasons why somebody might not work hard on a particular day," I said. "But you know, every week in the garden is a new week—you can start fresh anytime you choose. Next week

Perhaps the future does not lie in more and more complex methods of information transmission, but in the simple understanding that this planet is our home and that we live here thanks to a miraculous and complex web of life.

you could decide to come and be completely absorbed in the garden work." For a moment the boy sat reflecting, perhaps a little confused. Then to my surprise, he came across the circle to shake my hand, smiling broadly.

But as far as I am concerned, encouraging a strong work ethic is not a goal in itself. A few students work compulsively hard in the garden. One boy came to the garden and insisted on doing the heaviest work. He wheeled barrowload after barrowload of compost. (In the first year of the garden, the students added 70 tons of compost to the beds, using small wheelbarrows and shovels.) In this boy's case, the challenge was not to encourage him to work hard, but rather to help him develop other ways of being in the garden: hunting for the elusive squash hidden beneath a dense canopy of leaves, comparing the scent of the different varieties of basil we grow, or collecting edible flowers to garnish a salad.

For two girls who were very good at working with plants, the challenge was to make a trellis for our kiwi fruit, using tools and materials they were unfamiliar with. Over several weeks, they cut bay tree branches, dug holes, and experimented with different designs for building the structure. There was no plan for them to follow, and no expert showing them how things should be done. They did ask advice sometimes (but mainly they ignored a lot of unsolicited advice). It was a chance for them to create something they never before imagined being able to make with their own hands. Since the completion of the project, many people have commented on how beautiful it looks and have been surprised that such a sturdy and well designed structure was built by 12-year-old girls. Children need our respect. They benefit from challenges that make them feel as though they have made a contribution that goes far beyond getting good grades.

Encouraging the development of confidence entails a dance that gives young people the space to find their own way of doing things and familiarizing themselves with the elements they are working with in the garden. Much of this involves play—pure and simple. A lot of children have grown up without the chance to play in the sand, water, and mud, making dens or forts from branches, or even digging holes. Perhaps the future does not lie in more and more complex methods of information transmission, but in the simple understanding that this planet is our home, and that we live here thanks to a miraculous and complex web of life—sunlight, water, air, and all the plants and creatures that surround us. If children are going to care for the earth, then working and playing with the very stuff of existence is a priority. If they are going to be able to nourish and care for themselves and others, then learning the skills of growing and preparing food is an essential beginning.

Perhaps our most important task as adults is to learn how to respect and care for our young people. This is surely the best way to start helping them learn how to respect and care for the earth and the human community.

I am struck by the fact that the more slowly trees grow at first, the sounder they are at the core ... and I think the same is true of human beings.
We do not wish to see children precocious and making great strides in the early years, like sprouts, producing a soft and perishable timber, but better if they expand slowly at first as if contending with difficulties, and so are solidified and perfected. Such trees continue to expand with nearly equal rapidity to an extreme old age.

– The Journals of
 Henry David Thoreau

9

Digging Deeper in the School Garden

Planting Seeds for an Ecological Education

Developing methods to assess and evaluate the effectiveness of gardening projects and activities on children's learning, while labor-intensive, is essential for creating replicable and sustainable outdoor educational programs that genuinely work. In this chapter we discuss what we see as the deeper implications for using gardens as a springboard to fundamentally change the ways children learn in school, ways that are more ecologically-based, inquiry-driven, community-centered, and collaborative.

Chapter Nine outlines proven teaching methods for integrating youth gardening into an interdisciplinary school curriculum, including strategies for adapting gardening- and ecology-based programs to meet local, state, and national learning standards. While these topics will be particularly useful for teaching professionals, other garden organizers, parents, and community leaders will find a wealth of ideas here that are directly relevant to their work with children.

It has become increasingly apparent that among the most effective methods for inspiring children to take charge of their own learning are those that allow them rich opportunities to investigate the fabric of their everyday lives: by trying to understand how the world around them really works, starting in their own community, and by experiencing the mysteries of nature firsthand by growing their own food, as one example. Study after national study has shown what every parent and child has long known: children learn best from direct contact with the living world.

Across the country, more and more teachers are bringing their curriculum to life by reaching outside

> THE NEW GOLDEN RULE:
>
> EACH GENERATION SHOULD MEET ITS NEEDS WITHOUT JEOPARDIZING THE PROSPECTS OF FUTURE GENERATIONS TO MEET THEIR OWN NEEDS.[1]
>
> – Alan Durning,
> *How Much Is Enough*

the four walls of the classroom to find ways of covering "the basics" in nature and in the local community. This shift has been subtle and is hardly making headlines, but one by one, teachers are bringing the world of education out of the schoolroom, and not just through the Internet. A teacher might start by holding a science class out in the schoolyard. Another may begin with a small garden in the school courtyard. Perhaps another might take his or her class on a walk downtown to a senior citizens center or food shelf.

This is happening in every community, in every region, in every state and province. The fragile seeds for a truly community-based ecological education are being planted and tenderly nurtured as we educators all more deeply understand our lives as stewards and caretakers of the world that shapes our very being.

The challenge now is this: Do we have the courage and foresight to take the next step? Can we harness into a more unified voice the isolated initiatives to bring education out of the schoolroom, and move collectively to reconnect our education system back to the natural cycles that have sustained all societies since the beginning of time? Can we collectively take stock of the dramatic transformation of the natural environment wrought by progress and gather our shared resources to work toward a common goal of building humane and ecologically sound communities that will nourish all of life for future generations? Ultimately, that is the ambition of this book and of our work in schools.

Starting in the 1980s, Food Works set out to initiate interdisciplinary gardening programs in schools as one strategy for preventing childhood hunger, a quiet but growing crisis in Vermont in the face of increasing urbanization and the rapid loss of family farms. These one-shot enrichment programs, however, failed to engender any fundamental curricular change necessary for connecting the learning experience in school with the changing culture, interests, and needs of children in the wider community. This early work evolved into the Common Roots Program, a comprehensive curriculum development process aimed at transforming schools into local food and ecological research and resource centers. The key to this program's success has been a three-credit professional development course in which teachers draw on the unique cultural, ecological, and agricultural heritage of the surrounding community to develop their own local curriculum.

This chapter explains the rationale and methods for shaping such community-based curriculum units

K-6 HISTORICAL THEME GARDENS:

Social studies and science come to life for students in the garden. The Historic Theme Gardens™ invite students on a seven-year journey starting in their own back yard and moving through the agricultural history of their region, learning practical skills from the earliest Native American garden to the local community heritage culminating with the sustainable garden ecosystem of the future.

SAMPLE FRAMEWORK:

Grade K – Kinder Garden: ❶
The Earth-friendly "Kinder garden" is planted in sunflowers, carrots, and pumpkins.

Grades 1 & 2 – Native American Garden: ❷
Students plant corn, pole beans, and squash in a Native American garden. Under the "Wickiup" gardeners discover a great place to sit and watch the world.

Grade 3 – Community Heritage Garden: ❸
In the Community Heritage Garden elders and students work together planting, tending and harvesting crops from the community's past.

Grade 4 – Historical Garden: ❹
In the Historical Garden students grow heirloom varieties of crops once planted by the region's first settlers, such as wheat and oats, and experiment with antique gardening tools.

Grade 5 – Organic Kitchen Garden: ❺
Herbs, flowers and kitchen vegetables that were popular in early America are grown in the raised bed intensive garden.

Grade 6 – Sustainable Garden Ecosystem: ❻
Students apply sustainable garden practices with eyes towards answering the question: "How do we feed 6 billion people by the year 2000?"

All Grades – Market Garden: ❼
Throughout the summer student and family volunteers weed, thin and mulch the gardens. The market crops are then either sold to the community or donated to emergency food shelves.

K-6 Integrated Science Projects: Coupled with a study of China, sixth graders tend their indoor hydroponic fish-plant project similar to thousand-year-old Chinese models. This is an integrated food system with fish and plants prospering symbiotically and eventually producing an edible feast.

into a practical schoolwide framework that is readily understandable to students, teachers, parents, and the wider community. First, the relationship between schooling and the environment is discussed in light of the values and beliefs that have shaped modern education. Next, a step-by-step curriculum development process is spelled out demonstrating how Historic Theme Gardens provide a very practical means for reconnecting students to their natural and cultural roots.

By recreating the story of the community, these gardens become the living foundation for a grade-by-grade curriculum across the subject areas. Finally, to insure that all this hard work doesn't wind up as just another passing trend in the classroom but becomes deeply embedded in the culture of the community itself, five guiding principles are outlined for making change not just an annual event but a perennial cycle.

The indoor growing season parallels the planting themes of the outdoor gardens allowing for multiple harvests in the winter, integrating social studies, math, science, language, and creative arts.

SCHOOLYARD HABITATS

provide an opportunity for students to develop their skills in critical thinking, problem solving, and stewardship. Students apply their test results and insights in the form of newsletters, reports, presentations, and video's to the school and community. Older students share research using computers to telecommunicate on the RootsNet network.

SAMPLE FRAMEWORK:

A **Grade K – My Special Place:** *Students observe and record the changes "their" tree makes through the seasons.*

B **Grade 1 – The Forest Habitat:** *Students investigate adaptations, interdependence and change in the nearby forest.*

C **Grade 2 – The Meadow Thicket Habitat:** *Students investigate the diversity, adaptation and change of plants, animals, insects and birds.*

D **Grade 3 – The Soil Habitat:** *Students test and monitor soil samples from around their school, homes and community. They also maintain the school compost program.*

E **Grade 4 – The Water Habitat:** *Students study the interdependence of all life in the water. They test and evaluate the water quality of local samples and share their results with the school and community.*

F **Grade 5 – The Weather Station:** *Students monitor and forecast changes in weather conditions, compiling data for future uses and comparison.*

G **Grade 6 – The Earth Studies Station:** *Students monitor ecological changes such as acid rain, ozone depletion, climate change and network with regional, national and international organizations.*

Why Community-based Ecological Education?

LINKING EDUCATIONAL CHANGE TO ENVIRONMENTAL AND SOCIAL CHANGE—LOCALLY, NATIONALLY, GLOBALLY

"We cannot solve our problems with the same kind of thinking we used to create them," said Albert Einstein. As we edge into the 21st century, and the world's human population surpasses six billion, people across the planet are realizing that our very survival depends on understanding our relationship to the natural environment. Common sense dictates that any species that loses contact with and working knowledge of the sustaining organic world will decline and eventually die out.

From the voices of children everywhere come a deepening concern about the health of the earth, from the destruction of rain forests and the deterioration of the atmosphere globally, to overflowing regional landfills and dwindling supplies of pure water.

The litany of planetary ecological deterioration is now common knowledge, and needs no elaboration here beyond a few simple facts:

- More humans have been added to the world's total population in the past 40 years than in the previous three million years.[2]
- The earth loses 72 square miles of arable land per day to encroaching desert.[3]
- The Natural Research Council has estimated that as many as 8.8 million tons of oil end up in the ocean each year as a result of human activity.[4]
- According to the UN Food and Ag Organization, an estimated 70 percent of global fish stocks are over-exploited, fully exploited, depleted, or recovering from prior over-exploitation.[5]
- Today less than 5 percent of the original forest cover of the U.S. and Europe remains.[6]
- While nearly all the arable land in the U.S. is already in production, we are losing topsoil 18 times faster than it is being replaced while pumping water out of the ground 25 percent faster than it is being replenished.[7]

Add to this the increased chlorofluorocarbons in the atmosphere and rapid ozone depletion and it becomes clear that the planet's life-support system of air, water, and soil is in serious jeopardy.

Schools and the Environment

What does this dramatic transformation of the biosphere have to do with our educational system? How do schools reflect the values, attitudes, ways of thinking, and social structures that have fostered the economic, social, and political systems responsible for our gradual alienation from the natural world?

At their core, the methods and curriculum a society uses to teach its children mirror the fundamental values and beliefs of that society. The cultural and intellectual environment of schools, then, in a very real sense, creates the physical and natural environment around us. The basics we learn in school—A, B, C / 1, 2, 3—are the basics we see in the world.

In his path-breaking book, *Education and the Environment: Learning to Live with Limits*, Gregory Smith argues persuasively that how we think, and how we are taught to think in schools, will determine how we treat, or mistreat, our natural environment:

The disordering of ecological systems and of the great biogeochemical cycles of the earth reflects a prior disorder in the thought, perception, imagination, intellectual priorities, and loyalties inherent in the industrial mind. Ultimately, the ecological crisis concerns how we think and the institutions that purport to shape and refine the capacity to think.[8]

The way we learn about the world both reflects and recreates that world. An educational system that abstracts children from their home and divides the world into subjects that are taught in relative isolation will inevitably produce citizens who have difficulty recognizing the essential interconnectedness and interdependence of the human and natural world.

Indeed, a growing body of research is clearly showing how the roots of our ecological problems extend right to the heart of the rather fragmented, isolated way we learn about the world in school. Now, many administrators, teachers, and parents feel that traditional subject divisions may not be optimal for teaching children how to deal with endemic—and intimately related—social problems in today's world.

So what do we mean by "the basics" and "the real world"? What should be the most fundamental values, skills, and fields of knowledge that children should be learning in school? If teachers, administrators, and parents fully recognized the consequences of the slow but unmistakable deterioration of our natural environment, for example, then how would that change the structure, content, and methodologies of our modern industrial schools? In this paradigm, wouldn't "the basics" include learning essential skills and content in such "subjects" as food and nutrition studies, watershed studies, local natural and cultural history, community-service learning, and so on?

As schools embrace a more ecologically-focused context for teaching real-life experiences across the curriculum, children will increasingly be able to understand the essential connections between personal, local, national, and global issues. In its perennial attempt to reform itself into a more humane, democratic, and open institution, the American education system has a unique opportunity to recreate our schools to foster more integrated, holistic learning beginning in the immediate natural environment of the schools themselves.

A Change in Atmosphere?

Many current trends in school restructuring, however, have served mostly as a means for retooling students as workers in the new global economy. Almost totally absent from the discussions on school reform has been a critical discourse on the impact of the outcomes of our educational system on the planet's life-support systems that sustain us all.

Much of the current debate about educational standards and reforms, however, is driven by the belief that we must prepare the young only to compete effectively in the global economy. That done, all will be well, or so it is assumed. But there are better reasons to reform education which have to do with the rapid decline in the habitability of the earth. The kind of discipline-centric education that enabled us to industrialize the earth will not necessarily help us to heal the damage caused by industrialization.[9]

Around the country, public schools have been responding to these ecological concerns in three ways: Firstly, with isolated, one-shot activities such as a nature awareness exercise or an occasional environmental education field trip; secondly, through individual seasonal units with an environmental theme such as gardening, nature trails, and recycling; and thirdly, by

implementing comprehensive reforms that integrate practical, hands-on projects and activities, linking local natural and cultural history, community service, food growing, the arts, self-reflection exercises, and global environmental issues.

This third, more comprehensive approach has proven to be the most useful strategy both for teaching basic skills and for preparing the whole child to meet the social, economic, and ecological challenges of the 21st century.

If there is a growing need for this emerging holistic ecological approach to living and learning, then the question for every teacher and every school is: How do we begin adapting curriculum to nurture the inborn curiosity, natural wonder, and creative passion in every child, allowing them to find their own niche in the ecological web?

Educators are discovering the power of food and food growing as one key link between self, home, school, and community. Beyond basic nutrition and horticultural education, integrated school food programs are reconnecting students to the natural and cultural roots that have sustained human settlements over time. This practical teaching approach has proved to be an effective force for integrating traditionally separate academic subjects.

The rest of this chapter outlines the process for integrating gardening programs into a complete, community-based environmental curriculum that responds to the wide spectrum of needs and interests of the whole child.

Like the industrial model for agriculture, the industrial model of schooling is based on centralization, standardization, and specialization. It requires total loyalty to the twin gods of efficiency and effectiveness (as measured by "profits," which in education means the lowest possible monetary input for the largest number of young people processed through 12 years of schooling).

- **Centralization** moves the agenda for public schools out of rural communities, to the state and national level.
- **Standardization** (in textbook driven curriculum and national tests) severs students' ties to local areas, implying by neglect that they are unimportant because they are invisible.
- **Specialization** puts a premium on large numbers and substitutes quantity for any discussion of quality.

– Paul Nachtigal and Toni Haas, the National and Deputy Directors of the Annenburg Rural Challenge

Outgrowing Schools in the 21st Century

TRANSFORMING THE EXTRACTIVE MARKET GARDEN INTO THE REGENERATIVE GARDEN ECOSYSTEM

In many ways, our educational system can be looked at through the metaphor of a garden. On the one hand, modern schools are much like an annual market garden that extracts maximum yields with minimum input: Driven almost entirely by a short-term economic agenda, they are designed to produce students with marketable skills for sale to the highest bidder. This bottom-line way of thinking is founded largely on the belief that the continuous extraction of the earth's natural resources should be for the sole benefit of humans, with little regard for the other life forms that are essential to the stability of the overall system.

Cultivating a truly ecological education, on the other hand, is like nurturing a perennial garden in which the cultivars yield a continuous harvest in harmony with their natural surroundings, benefitting the soil, insects, birds, wildlife, and all species of the larger natural community.

The following chart illustrates the contrast between a modern education and an ecological education in the areas of theory, process, and product.

Ways of Thinking (Theory)

CONTEMPORARY EDUCATION (The Extractive Market Garden)	ECOLOGICAL EDUCATION (The Regenerative Garden Ecosystem)
Separation: The individual self is autonomous and separate from the rest of the world.	*Interdependence*: Humans are inseparable from and interdependent with life in the biotic communities in which they live.
Domination: Humans are the world's dominant species with a divine right to harvest any and all of the earth's natural resources for their own happiness and prosperity.	*Cooperation*: As creatures in the vast and intricate web of life, humans are ultimately shaped and governed by the same ecological principles as every other species.
Material Progress: Society advances through a series of technological innovations based on rational, scientific theoretical models.	*Sustainability*: An ecosystem sustains itself by continuously recycling water, air, and nutrients, which support an ever-growing diversity of interdependent species.
Infinite Growth: Not only are there no limits to growth, but when expansion is slowed or curtailed, the system is viewed as failing.	*Natural Limits*: Each ecosystem has its own limited carrying capacity, which is a natural function of climate, geology, biodiversity, and human impact.
Omnipotence: Humans have the capacity to thoroughly understand and master all of the earth's natural cycles and to manage any irregularity in those cycles that may arise, humanly caused or otherwise.	*Integration*: Each species is able to find its unique niche in the larger ecosystem only by following basic ecological principles that shape the larger biotic community, instinctively honoring its essential connection with the natural environment.

Ways of Learning (Process)

MARKET-DRIVEN CURRICULUM	ECOLOGICALLY-DRIVEN CURRICULUM
The Basics—reading, writing and arithmetic to learn skills for becoming proficient in the market economy	The Basics—ecological awareness, stewardship, and restoration to become literate in the watershed ecology
Instruction focused on nationally driven academic standards	Instruction guided by ecological principles reflecting each unique watershed
Isolated, abstract subjects	Practical integrated themes in a continuum of earth stewardship
Four-walled classrooms are the best place to learn	We are part of a community of learners, with nature as our teacher and guide
Accountability: Data-driven results comparing individual students, schools, states, and countries by quantifying logical, mathemetical, and linguistic skills	Accountability: The health, vitality, and diversity of all species in a given region is the primary indicator of a community's ecological literacy
Preparation and training for the Global Economy	Care and respect for the earth, locally and globally

Ways of Being (Product)

MARKET-DRIVEN CURRICULUM	ECOLOGICALLY-DRIVEN CURRICULUM
Segmentation	Integration
Competition	Cooperation
Complacency, boredom	Curiosity, enchantment
Institutionalized roles, responsibilities	Ecological niche, purpose
Personal alienation	Instinctive connection
Independence	Interdependence

This schematic was inspired by an article in *Green Teacher* magazine, Fall, 1997, entitled "Paradigms Lost" by Mark McElroy of the Hartland, Vermont School Board.

Educational Tools for a Holistic Curriculum

A STEP-BY-STEP PROCESS FOR DEVELOPING A COMMUNITY-BASED SCHOOL GARDENING PROGRAM

How can a school garden become the catalyst for an integrated curriculum based on a Pedagogy of Place, linking home, school, and community? Educators aiming to create meaningful lesson plans and year-round learning units around gardening typically focus on these three areas:

A. **THEORY:** guiding questions and the search for alternatives for teaching and learning in a sustainable way

B. **CURRICULUM DEVELOPMENT PROCESS:** connecting gardening programs to an integrated school-wide framework based on the community story
   - Common Roots Journey
   - Project Web
   - Historic Theme Gardens

C. **COMMUNITY INVOLVEMENT:** broadening participation

A. Theory: The Search for Alternatives

The effectiveness (of a given pedagological activity) depends on the extent to which adults are clear in their understanding of the ideological underpinnings of this pedagogy.

–Elizabeth Cagan, from Jesse Goodman Brown, "Change Without Difference"

Through a decade of Food Works' collaboration with teachers, a body of questions has emerged regarding the ideals and values that underlie the curriculum in modern schools. Increasingly, teachers are interested in exploring how these philosposhical issues can shed light on the challenges posed by the overwhelming needs of children today. This sampling of some of the more compelling questions that we have heard from teachers around the country provides a useful context for identifying the ideological foundations for school curriculum:

- Are schools adequately responding to the academic, social, emotional, psychological, physical, economic, and ecological needs of children today?
- What do children need to learn to lead healthy, happy, ecologically sustainable lives?
- What is the role and responsibility of schools in meeting those needs?
- How can teachers develop meaningful curricula to respond to these diverse needs of children?
- What kinds of jobs should schools be preparing children for that address their social and economic needs and those of their communities?
- Are schools fostering strong connnections between home, family, and community as part of their curriculum?

Joseph Kiefer, the co-founder and Education Director of Food Works, initiated the Common Roots curriculum development process in 1990 to fully integrate gardening and ecological studies into a community-based school curriculum. The Common Roots program is launched in schools through a three-credit professional development course for teachers that is taught by Food Works teaching associates. Taught on-site, this course draws from the local natural and cultural heritage to create integrated learning units aligned to district, state, and national standards.

- What does our school teach about local history, culture, and the natural environment to develop a meaningful sense of place in children?
- How do we develop a community-based pedagogy to guide us in building an education that meets the needs of all children into the 21st century, while sustaining our natural heritage?

When teachers at a specific school ask themselves these questions, they begin a conversation about the importance of the history, ecology, and traditions that are unique to each locality. Following this first stage of the inquiry comes the development of a community profile, identifying the needs, strengths, and challenges of students, the school, and the wider community. The findings of this community/school profile direct the development of a schoolwide framework, consisting of interdisciplinary study units in food, ecology, and community.

B. The Curriculum Development Process

The Common Roots curriculum development process developed by Food Works enables teachers to recreate their community's story through a professional development graduate course exploring five basic questions.

Where are we?

Course work begins with retelling the story of the community by asking this simple question: Where are we geographically, ecologically, historically, demographically, and culturally? At this early stage, an area historian is often invited to participate, along with various elders, to share passed-down stories about the local history, skills, wisdom, traditional knowledge, folklore, and changes to the land over time.

Who are we?

This is a detailed look at the needs, strengths, and challenges of the school, students, families, and the local environment, as part of the community/school profile. This stage culminates in a wide-ranging discussion of the implications of this profile for teaching and learning. For example, if 40 percent of a school's population are receiving free or reduced lunches, what are the needs of these children and their families and what kinds of meaningful learning opportunities can be provided for them? How do we respond to their immediate and longer-term needs?

What are we doing?

This focuses on the existing school culture: the curriculum, teaching methods, content, standards, assessment tools, and professsional development course work. This includes thematic studies about food, the environment, community-service learning, and opportunities for parent and community involvement. An additional task at this stage is to identify the natural and cultural resources that exist locally and to create a plan for integrating them into the curriculum. Does the school have a focal point(s) that gives it a unique identity, such as school gardens or a living arts program?

Where can we go?

What do we need to know to live here sustainably? What is the vision for transforming the school into a center for community learning that addresses the relevant needs of students, families, and the community? How do we educate children while at the same time enhance the habitability of this watershed for future generations? How do we find our own unique niche in the local ecosystem? How do we apply the traditional knowledge passed down from elders to our everyday lives? How can we use school grounds to re-invigorate a natural and agricultural heritage by growing foods from the past (indigenous and traditional American food systems), foods of today (backyard garden and community food systems), and intensive food production for the future (an organic sustainable food system)?

At this stage, the group develops a vision statement describing the specific plans of the indoor and outdoor educational landscape. How can our schools become true community resource centers for research, education, and demonstration, working toward food and ecological security for all?

How do we get there?

What skills, knowledge, activities, methods, and standards are needed to teach in a more ecologically sustainable way? What is our action plan and time line for implementing the Common Roots Framework by recreating the story of the community as a living curriculum? What standards should be set for children to insure their understanding and support of an ecologically sustainable future?

Once this framework has been developed, there will be a clearer picture of local history, geography, ecology, and demographics. With this understanding of place and needs, teachers are ready to identify agricultural and ecological thematic areas for building a grade-by-grade curriculum of practical, hands-on learning.

Designing the Schoolwide Framework.

Food Works' strategy for building a Pedagogy of Place requires teachers to create a grade-by-grade story following the near-to-far social studies framework already in place in schools throughout much of the world. This framework provides a consistent developmental foundation for telling a story unique to each community. The near-to-far social studies approach has proved an ideal vehicle, both for telling the local story through the grades and for making that story relevant to stu-

dents, teachers, and the community. Developing different historic gardens for each grade allows teachers to link their existing social studies themes—Native Americans, European explorers, the local community, regions of the U.S.—by creating a logical, historical progression for these units that parallels the agricultural history of the community.

For example, kindergartners enter school by exploring their garden and nature as it relates to the self. Grades one and two look at the indigenous peoples of their community as part of the first homes and neighborhoods. Grades three and four create a community heritage garden to bring to life regional and state history. Grades five and six explore the sustainable garden ecosystem as it relates to U.S. and world history, grappling with more complex global issues such as, how do we feed over six billion people in the 21st century?

The major Thematic Areas of the grade-by-grade developmental framework are based on the answers to the five driving questions: Where are we? Who are we? What are we doing? Where can we go? How do we get there? Examples of Thematic Areas that teachers have adopted include: Historic Theme Gardens, Schoolyard Habitats, Community-service Learning, Entrepreneurial Opportunities, Stories from our Elders, Celebrations and Festivals, and Appropriate Technologies.

Teams of teachers from various subjects and age levels then chart their lessons based on local seasonal variations, tying together their Thematic Areas into a logical sequence. As they develop the program, teachers incorporate the grade-appropriate district and state curriculum standards to each Thematic Area. This insures that the prescribed content in traditional subject areas mandated by the district and state is addressed through these explorations and discoveries in the indoor and outdoor educational landscape.

C. Community Involvement: Broadening Participation

Recreating the story of the student's own community provides an ideal context for meaningful learning. The teacher can say to children just entering school: "Each season we are going on an adventure to live the lives of the people who first lived here. We are going to follow in their footsteps and learn from their lessons—how they survived and sustained themselves over time. We will discover what foods they grew and how they grew them. We will explore how they experienced and harnessed nature in balance or out of balance, constructively or destructively. We will experience their culture, arts, dance, theater, and music.

"We will walk in these woods and meadows, and learn what grows here and what animals live here. We will learn about the houses and neighborhoods and families that have built this town over the generations. We will meet the people who live here, talk to the elders, to the men and women who went to school in this place, to hear their stories and concerns and questions. This is the starting point for your formal education."

These, then, are the three basic elements for cultivating a Pedagogy of Place: food literacy, ecological literacy, and cultural literacy. As an old farmer once said during a harvest meal at one of our Common Roots schools, "If you don't know where you came from, how can you know where you're going?"

The Common Roots Journey

Grade	Integrated Science Theme Question(s)	Developmental Social Studies Theme	Historic Theme Garden	School Yard Habitat
K	What do we and all living things need to survive?	Self	"Kinder Garden"	My Special Place
1	How do all living things fulfill their needs in nature?	Home	Three Sisters Native American Garden	The Forest
2	How do all living things adapt to fit their habitat/environment? What is the interrelationship between all living things and their environment?	Neighborhood	Farmers and Gardeners of the Longhouse	The Meadow Thicket
3	How do all natural and human communities change over time? What can we learn from our community heritage that will help sustain us in the future?	Community	Community Heritage Garden	The Soil Community
4	How has the climate of our region/state effected the historical diet of the inhabitants? What role has water played in the historical development of our region?	Region/State	Colonial Garden	The Watershed
5	How does climate determine the composition of a region's living communities and land forms (biomes)?	Country	Organic Kitchen Gardens in Early U.S. History	Weather Station
6	How are all living and non-living components of the earth interrelated?	World	Sustainable Garden Ecosystem	Earth Studies Station

Project Webs: Reweaving the Web of Learning through the Garden

Anyone who has taught gardening in school knows how challenging it is to contain garden activities to any one discipline. The art and science of gardening naturally leads students from doing the basic math involved in layout and design; to understanding natural science and the ecology of the immediate environment in deciding what to plant and where to plant it; to studying health and nutrition basics when harvest time comes; and on to journaling and poetry and storytelling and to the living arts including painting, drama, music, and crafts.

This sample integrated project web illustrates how a historic theme garden cultivates meaningful learning activities across the disciplines. The web illustrates how the skills and content areas that teachers are required to cover on the state and district

"**YOU'RE SUPPOSED TO BE COVERING THE BASICS. WHAT ARE YOU DOING OUTDOORS GARDENING?**"

level can be achieved through a unified focus helping students to more fully understand the natural connections between traditionally isolated subjects.

The thematic garden web shown here has the additional advantage of anchoring the disciplines in a sense of place by focusing horticultural activities on the unique agricultural heritage of each region. In addition to learning the basic math and science of growing food, flowers, and herbs, students also discover that historic theme gardens such as the Three Sisters Garden bring context and meaning to the social studies story of their community, which includes conducting research, collecting oral histories, writing reports, and making presentations. Such an integrated study engenders an ecology of thinking where the lines that separate one discipline from another dissolve and the essential connections between the fields of knowledge are more deeply understood.

A cross-curriculum webbing process is particularly helpful to teachers when applied to other aspects of curriculum planning.

Project Web

What can be discovered in the Three Sisters Garden?

SCIENCE / ECOLOGY
Plant identification
Plant biology
Garden ecosystem
Insect identification
Weather patterns
Effects of moonlight
Effects of sunlight
Earth's rotation

MATH
Average yield of crops
Volume & weight
 of seeds & produce
Graphing
Charting
Symmetry
Recipes

**NUTRITION &
HEALTH**
Food groups
Cooking
Food preservation
Drying vegetables

SOCIAL STUDIES
Iroquois Indian Nation
History of corn
Native American foods

GARDENING
Design
Preparation
Compost
pH
Cover crops
Seed storage
Germinate seeds
Mulch

LANGUAGE ARTS
Harvest songs
Native American stories
Poetry
Write and tell stories
Journal entries

CREATIVE ARTS
Harvest mural
Make cookbook
Draw plants
Dibble sticks
Journal drawings
Costume making
Puppets
Plays

COMMUNITY SERVICE
Donate soup
Corn gifts
Cookbook gifts
Share harvest
Displays & exhibits
Gifting Garden Ceremony
Three Sisters
 Harvest Celebration

Historic Theme Gardens

A SAMPLE THEMATIC AREA FOR RECREATING THE COMMUNITY'S STORY

Standards-based assessment webs can be created, for example, by listing directly underneath each activity the district standards that are to be assessed and, eventually, met by completing the activity (or activities).

Curriculum webs can be applied to any line of inquiry that students share: Around gardening, it can be adapted to explore the first settlers to an area (indigenous), plus colonial, contemporary, and even sustainable gardens of the future. The process is also useful for webbing out integrated activities around themes that go much further afield, including geography, technology, sports, astronomy, and virtually any other topic that might interest a group of students, young or old.

This basic curriculum organizing tool demonstrates to administrators as well as to parents and community members how focusing learning activities on thematic gardens catalyzes practical, real-world learning which students can use for a lifetime.

After all, what could be more basic than a garden?

In keeping with the natural ecological sensibility that has sustained so many indigenous societies over time, Historic Theme Gardens offer students opportunities to follow in the footsteps of those who have come before.

All students can learn the story of their community by retracing the patterns of human settlement through the creation of their own Historic Theme Gardens. Who were the first peoples to live here? What was their diet and their relationship to the natural world and to one another? How have shifting settlement patterns affected the landscape, the people, and the culture over time?

By conducting this agricultural research, students gain firsthand insight into the tools, techniques, and food ways of earlier inhabitants of the same watershed. As the changing methods of local food-growing through history is understood, the foundation for a community's Historic Theme Garden design gradually takes shape. This moves local history from the abstract in a textbook to a real-life experience. By telling the story of each community's agricultural legacy, Historic Theme Gardens become a living testimony to a vanishing heritage.

These gardens are powerful vehicles for hands-on learning because children are naturally drawn to and deeply curious about the wonders of all living things, especially when they cultivate that life themselves.

For many children it is their first chance to have contact with and responsibility for something alive. With carefully planned seasonal investigations, the Historic Theme Garden can nourish the curiosity of children throughout the year.

Using food in daily lesson plans reinforces and adds meaning to the overall story of a community. Students can go back in time using traditional regional recipes for cooking and baking activities. Nutrition takes on new meaning when students have their own garden and eat foods that they may have never tasted before.

During the cold months, an indoor garden provides students with daily contact with plants. Growing lettuce, beans, tomatoes, and radishes indoors gives children year-round access to fresh, healthy, nutritious foods. Classroom earthworm farms are also excellent tools for learning soil science, the life cycles of worms, and the decomposition process.

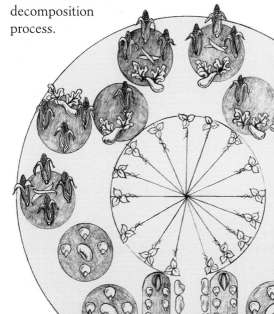

Digging in for the Long Haul

FIVE BASIC PRINCIPLES FOR SUSTAINING A SCHOOL GARDENING PROGRAM

There is no simple formula for transforming schools into community learning centers using sound ecological principles through gardening. Indeed, Food Works' own "transitional tool kit" of curriculum development strategies is continually changing as parents and educators from communities around the country adapt their own unique earth-centered approaches to teaching and learning. Through all the changes and adaptations, however, we always return to this same organizing principle:

> To sense ourselves to be one with the world, surely, awakening that realization must be a central task for an education which would heal the fractures wrought by our disassociation from other life forms with whom we share this small planet.[10]

Each week, Food Works receives phone calls from teachers, principals, school board members, parents, and students across the U.S. and Canada, requesting our practical, community-based teaching tools. This growing demand demonstrates that these kinds of programs can assist schools and communities in producing more creative, passionate, and self-motivated children for the tremendous challenges of the future.

In order to do this, and to make programs last, we have identified five principles for keeping a youth gardening program going strong in schools.

1. Recognize the enormous ecological changes of our time, locally and globally.

Firstly, educators, together with the community at large, must recognize the massive ecological changes in their own region and the entire planet over the past century. Furthermore, it is critical to acknowledge the role of our educational system in this process. This central issue should be the focus of school change and community development. Linking education and ecology at the very outset of the curriculum development process provides schools with a real-world context for learning to take place, and builds the foundation for holistic education.

2. Emphasize community-based learning, especially in the early grades.

It is crucial for schools to focus curriculum locally, even if using resources, teaching materials, and lesson plans that come from far away. Learning the basics in the context of their own community makes students more eager to take responsibility for their own education. At the same time, they learn to value the place where they live. If lessons disregard local history, homes, and habitats, children are less likely to be concerned about the fate of their natural heritage and the rest of the world.

3. Unify curriculum through the use of story.

Unifying different subjects through the unique story of each community is a powerful tool. Not only does a story help locate each teacher's disparate units along a logical continuum, but a local story also draws in parents and community members, honoring local wisdom and institutions.

Theologian Thomas Berry speaks of the power of story to give meaning to our lives:

> For peoples generally, their story of the universe and the human role in the universe is their primary source of intelligibility and value. ... It communicates the most sacred of mysteries. ... The deepest crises experienced by any society are those moments of change when the story becomes inadequate for meeting the survival demands of the present situation. Such, it seems to me, is the situation we must deal with in this late twentieth century.[11]

4. Plan collaborative teaching.

As a catalyst for change, teachers should plan, design, and implement their curriculum collaboratively. Developing consistent unifying themes makes learning more meaningful. To address the issue of collaboration at the microlevel, traditional walls that separate teachers and subjects must come down, so faculty can work together cooperatively—as part of the normal school day.

Our on-the-job research has shown that closer collaboration enables teachers to set an example of the kinds of communication and cooperation that they are trying to cultivate in children while meeting the unique developmental needs of the students.

5. Remain open to the vast changes we are all undergoing, collectively and individually.

As we develop more earth-centered ways of teaching and learning, it is only natural to find, in ourselves as well as others, some fear, resistance, and anxiety. Questioning the dominant story and myths upon which our society and economy are founded can be a very difficult process that challenges our personal sense of security.

More people are finding, though, that this questioning process can be both healthy and good as we collectively reestablish our intuitive connection to nature and to one another. This process of questioning and change demands courage and strength in order to transcend the conventional patterns of learning taught not only by schools, but also by society at large. Invariably, however, letting go of past patterns becomes more compelling—personally, professionally, socially—as we experience how these old routines, habits, and ways of thinking are physically and spiritually exhausting while failing to nurture ourselves or our planet.

Increasingly, educators recognize nature as a powerful teacher in both content and method. By incorporating nature into our teaching, we are free to discover the vital life force that exists in each of us, in the land itself, and in every family, neighborhood, community, and bioregion. The challenge is to allow this natural impulse to take form in our everyday lives and to make this learning our lifelong curriculum.

NOTES:

1. Durning, Alan. 1992. *How Much Is Enough? The Consumer Society and the Future of the Earth*. New York: W.W. Norton

2. *Wild Earth* magazine, Winter 1997/98, p. 16

3. Orr, David. 1994. *Earth in Mind*. Washington, D.C.: Island Press.

4. *E Magazine*, January/February 1998, p. 31

5. *E Magazine*, January/February 1998, p. 30

6. *WorldWatch* magazine, January/February 1998, p. 1

7. *Wild Earth* magazine, Winter 1997/98, p. 91

8. Smith, Greg. 1992. *Education and the Environment*. Albany: SUNY Press.

9. Orr, David. 1994. *Earth in Mind*. Washington, D.C: Island Press.

10. Kesson, Kathleen. 1995. Paper delivered at "Education for a Green World Conference." Rutland, Vermont.

11. Berry, Thomas. 1988. *The Dream of the Earth*. San Francisco: Sierra Books

10

Nature as Teacher

A Greenprint for Ecologically Sustainable Cultures

Imagine for a moment that all the hopes and aspirations for a genuine children's gardening movement in communities across North America actually became realized as we have spelled them out in this guide.

Suppose that the existing children's gardens—those organized by 4-H clubs and summer rec programs and families in their own backyards—were genuinely honored as living examples of a return to the natural cycles of the earth.

Imagine that these small individual efforts grew to include not only cultivating food, but also learning nutrition basics (with vitamin gardens); eating homegrown food (daily salad bars and community harvest meals); cooking and baking (fresh garden pizza); donating local produce (to area food shelves); selling locally grown foods (at the farmers' market); putting food by (youth-made salsa and sweet pickles); saving seeds (local heirloom preservation); strengthening the regional food system (school lunch foods from local farms and community composting bins); celebrating the arts (mid-summer garden festivals); and honoring local traditions and cultural heritage (elders sharing stories, food varieties, and recipes from their childhoods).

Suppose that these gardening efforts expanded into childcare programs, senior centers, hospitals, and schools that adapted year-round garden-based curriculum using indoor and outdoor gardens.

Imagine that a garden in every school grew into a garden in every grade, incorporating an integrated food education program for teaching local history, science, math, language, and creative arts in meaningful and lasting ways that benefitted the entire community.

A THING IS RIGHT WHEN IT TENDS TO PRESERVE THE INTEGRITY, STABILITY AND BEAUTY OF THE BIOTIC COMMUNITY. IT IS WRONG WHEN IT TENDS OTHERWISE.

– Aldo Leopold,
A Sand County Almanac

When all this has come to pass—when towns, cities, and neighborhoods have decided to make food and the environment a primary focus for community learning—will this be enough? Or is this just the beginning?

The Limits to Environmental Thinking

To what extent can simply gardening with children address the multitude of needs that children have today? How can the basic pleasures of a garden ever compete with the glamour and glitz of media technologies like movies, television, and video games? Living in a world almost completely constructed by humans, how can we use a garden to find our place in the biotic community? How do children have a chance to appreciate history and their own heritage in a world so fascinated and preoccupied by the future? How can we be expected to honor our elders living in a youth-obsessed culture? How can children cultivate an ethic of sustainability in a school system that consistently fails to teach and reward teamwork? How can our current educational system incorporate a garden into its traditional 50-minute routine? Can gardens alone really change the larger cultural curriculum?

These questions point to the most troubling challenges that we all must face in determining how to shape schools and the wider society to be more responsive to and responsible toward the natural world on which we all depend.

Living in such a highly technological society, we seem to have lost the language of the land as we become further and further removed from an ancestral heritage that once had a highly sophisticated system of living and commuicating with the natural world.

Youth gardening programs, however well-intentioned, will only take root in schools and communities when they explicitly address these most pressing social and ecological issues facing all of us into the 21st century. Rather than be mere add-ons to a pre-determined, market-driven curriculum, children's gardens can be catalysts for cultivating an ethics of stewardship and cooperation that offers a fundamentally different orientation to the environment, the economy, and society than that which has traditionally been fostered in schools.

Increasingly, the most promising literature from advanced educational scholars recognizes the crucial link between current educational reform efforts, contemporary values, and the state of the environment.

Dr. Chet Bowers from Oberlin College, for example, has observed:

> *If the thinking that guides educational reform does not take account of how the cultural beliefs and practices passed on through schooling relate to the deepening ecological crisis, then these efforts may actually strengthen the cultural orientation that is undermining the sustaining capacities of natural systems upon which all life depends.*

Bowers, C.A. *Education, Cultural Myths and the Ecological Crisis.*

Efforts to initiate a comprehensive "ecological education" will prevail only when they are driven by a clear understanding of the relationship between the present

From Bus Depots and Garages to Gardens and Greenhouses

In 1987, a bus garage was demolished next to Junior High School 60 on New York City's Lower East Side, leaving a vacant lot with toxic soil contaminated by old petroleum. As controversy grew in the neighborhood over the lot's development and what to do with the toxic soil, teachers and administrators from the school, together with a local non-profit organization called Open Road, organized public meetings and distributed surveys to parents, students, teachers, and neighbors. Surveys showed most people wanted one-third of the lot to be a garden and two-thirds to be a playground.

In 1993, the group joined with the East Side Community High School and signed a Green Thumb lease for the property, receiving permission to develop a garden on the site. Soon thereafter, they received funding and a landfill liner from the Department of Sanitation to cap the contaminated soil in the garden area. Next, they organized volunteer workdays and raised additional money to hire a landscape architect, rent bulldozers, and buy gravel and soil to spread over the liner.

All three schools in the adjacent school building have been involved in the design and development of the space and hold regular science, language, math, and art classes in the garden for grades seven through 12. Students, staff, and volunteers designed and built a compost-heated greenhouse, a fish and turtle pond, a solar-powered waterfall, murals, grape arbors, tree mounds with evergreen and fruit trees, intensive organic vegetable beds, herb gardens, organic lawns, and bird and butterfly habitats. The project has become a model of community and student design, and is used for city-wide teacher workshops. In addition, the students' maps, models, and completed projects have inspired design and environmental education curriculum now being used in 18 other schools in New York City.

The seeds for a renaissance have been broadcast throughout Gotham, and the ecological revolution will not be televised!

state of the environment and the values and beliefs that shape contemporary schooling.

Gardening and exploring nature with children offer us the challenge of digging deeper to recover ways of knowing that are directly attuned to the earth's life-support systems. Our task is nothing less than having to *re*-form our schools to reflect these age-old teachings that honor the essential interconnectedness and oneness of all of life. How could we ever hope to cultivate such an orientation again?

In today's schools, the prescription for including the environment in the learning process generally follows the conventional three-step formula: awareness, knowledge, and action.

1. **Awareness:** First, learners must have opportunities to gain firsthand sensory experiences of the environment, stimulating their natural curiosity and sense of wonder.
2. **Knowledge:** From this awareness grows a more focused inquiry process inspired by the learners' desires to investigate the living world that surrounds them.
3. **Action:** By experiencing the natural sciences and natural history of the land, students become motivated to participate in an informed and purposeful way in stewardship and restoration of their immediate environment.

As effective as this approach has been for getting children outdoors, it has generally failed to change the modern orientation toward the natural environment as something outside of and separate from humanity. Indeed, environmental education programs have almost universally been implemented only to supplement a core curriculum of traditionally unconnected subjects.

As a society, we have seen how this abstract method of teaching serves to reinforce the values, knowledge, and skills for increased industrialization and economic growth, using the environment as a natural resource to promote progress. Teaching "environmental studies" as an occasional enrichment of the conventional disciplines is itself a classic example of how we have tried to separate ourselves from nature in order to use it for our own purposes. Even the best environmental education will fall short if it fails to address the underlying assumptions and beliefs that shape this modern world view.

A true ecological education involves a fundamental reorientation of the human role in the biotic community from one of separateness and domination to one of integration and interdependence. Simply reforming the modern industrial school every 10 to 20 years will not change the underlying cultural assumption that sees schools as mere training programs for occupations in a growth-oriented economy, an economy that treats the environment as little more than fuel for the engines of expansion.

As a species, humans have millions of years of accumulated ecological wisdom woven into the core of our very being, and a mere 500 or so years of scientific-industrial knowledge piling up in our cultural database. Which should we choose as the most reliable foundation for nurturing future generations in harmony with the living world? How do we root our learning in the deepest and most sustainable ways of knowing that are available to us? How can we find a natural balance between these seemingly disparate ways of knowing?

Finding Equilibrium Where We Are

The obvious starting point is to look where we already live. The signs of a new equilibrium are everywhere. In every community across this diverse and bounteous land, seeds are sprouting, gardens are growing, local habitats are being explored, and curriculums are being rewritten. Indeed, the growth of every flower, every child, and every garden is an integral step toward a more ecological way of living and learning.

Identifying this starting point of equilibrium, then, naturally begins in an open place in the present moment. Such an openness is itself at the very heart of cultivating this simple awareness that is so crucial for attuning to the elemental wisdom of the earth. Out of this awareness of where we are, we can start to see the patterns, shapes, and cycles in our own lives that mirror the natural ecosystem in which we live. By drawing from these primary images, we begin to forge the necessary links to recreate this balance, this primordial integration between human and natural systems.

The following Greenprint is a sequence of strategies for reclaiming our rightful place in the biotic world. The four primary areas or dimensions of the Greenprint aim to reconnect our collective learning process to the everyday lessons of nature in our own homes, neighborhoods, communities, and bioregions.

Nature's Greenprint

Four Dimensions to Building Sustainable Communities

As a society now entering a new millennium, we are at last gaining a much clearer sense of the inherent limits to the current industrial model of progress. With this deeper understanding, we are beginning to identify those wellsprings of an ecological education that can shape the theory, methods, and content for guiding a community of learners. The challenge now is to integrate the wildly diverse aspects of ecological learning into a holistic framework that is deeply rooted in the all-encompassing natural heritage that is our perennial teacher.

The four dimensions that form this Greenprint follow the sequential steps of conventional environmental education—Ecological Awareness, Ecological Knowledge, and Ecological Action, with a fourth

To know is to

remember.

– Plato

dimension woven into the tapestry that connects them all, Ecological Consciousness. This framework endeavors to draw from the strengths of traditional environmental thinking and integrate them into a deeper ecological consciousness that honors humans' essential nature as biological creatures who depend on the land.

Through this process of remembering—both our instinctive sense of belonging to a specific place and our innate connection to others who share this primal connection to the earth—we are invoking the same natural consciousness that we have shared with other species for millennia. This consciousness becomes the integral driving force that continually informs our relationships to each other and to all living beings.

To Look at Any Thing

To look at any thing,
If you know that thing,
You must look at it long:
To look at this green and say
"I have seen spring in these
woods," will not do—you must
Be the thing you see:
You must be the dark snakes of
Stems and ferny plumes of leaves,
You must enter in
to the small silences between
The leaves
You must take your time
And touch the very peace
They issue from.

– John Moffitt

Dimension One: Ecological Awareness

Children are born naturalists. They leave the womb with an instinctive sense of the natural world. Watch infants crawling on grass: notice their fascination with a simple stone, a single blade of grass, a solitary leaf. Now watch their reaction when a fidgety squirrel, a twittering bird, or a curious dog crosses their field of vision. Filled with awe, they intuitively reach out to contact these strange, but familiar beings. After a year passes, see how their curiosity has grown. They begin to ask, What? How? Where? Why?, instinctively exploring and asking questions about the world of which they are an essential part.

Awareness of our environment is as basic to our nature as breathing. The only prerequisite for nurturing this awareness is the conscious desire to put it at the forefront of our learning process. This innate curiosity then becomes the most powerful force for attuning to the source of our natural instincts.

A first step for concerned educators is to take time to be alone in nature and to allow that subtle awareness to become the focus of our attention. A key to this process is allowing ample opportunity to reflect on the feelings, images, and insights that arise from simply finding a place to be still and observe. Focusing attention provides both a living example and a conscious environment for students of any age to explore the natural world and to find their niche in it.

The process of becoming aware becomes a self-perpetuating cycle. The more aware we become of our world, the more we experience that world, and in turn the more aware we become of what we experience. Like throwing a pebble into a pond, concentric circles of awareness grow ever outward as we extend our reach into the growing universe. Awareness is the first ripple of understanding into the ever-changing pond of ecological knowledge, action, and consciousness.

Dimension Two: Ecological Knowledge

Go and learn from indigenous people because they are the last reservoirs of knowledge of how to live sustainably with the environment. – 1987 Brundtland Report

Communities are inherently ecological. Human beings have long been students of their environment, with a working knowledge and fundamental appreciation of the watersheds in which they have roamed—including the local topography, plants, trees, animals, waterways, and weather patterns. The "basics" of this day-to-day ecological study have involved reading the landscape, gathering wild foods, tracking game, judging distances, gauging changes in the weather, estimating carrying capacity, and communicating this information among themselves.

Over time, the original inspiration for these primal learning experiences was gradually adapted into more formalized subject areas of modern academic curriculum, though obviously in a very different context. This ancient study—learning how to live in a particular place—forms the foundation for an integrated, earth-centered curriculum.

Gaining sustenance from the land depends on having an everyday understanding of the sources of food, water, medicine, shelter, and clothing available in the immediate environment. In indigenous societies, and increasingly in pockets of modern society as well, people have developed an intimate relationship with their local flora and fauna. They have learned the wild plants that can be harvested for food and used for healing and medicine; the trees that are appropriate for shelter, fuel, fruits, and nuts; and the animals that can be sacrificed for meat, clothing, and tools.

These native and non-native species are themselves the teachers, providing lessons in basic principles like adaptation, interdependence, reciprocity, sustainability, respect, compassion, and purposefulness. They also teach that all living things have their own essence and unique niche. The natural world, then, offers a classroom filled with the practical wisdom, "learned" over millions of years, of how to find and maintain a dynamic balance with other species on this planet.

When we say earth in our language, we don't mean just the physical earth but rather something you might call energy. ... [Over time that] knowledge became fragmented. This ancient knowledge will rise again, only this time the key to it is integration.

– Pamela Colorado, Wayfinding in the New Sun: Indigenous Science in the Modern World

An essential characteristic of ecological knowledge is that the learner is an inseparable part of what is being learned. We *are* nature. Everything we do is inextricably connected to the life-support systems of the earth. Therefore, ecological knowledge is human knowledge and must be properly integrated into the communities that value education as a key element to their long-term health and well-being.

If a community endeavors to reconnect its learning to the ecological story of its own watershed as it has been passed down (and which is as available in contemporary cultures as it is in the teachings of the earth itself), then the learners' inquiry can be guided along thematic units of study that correspond to the local topography, climate, flora, fauna, and waterways.

GETTING STARTED WITH FOOD STUDIES

When food is no longer associated with farming and with the land, then the eaters are suffering a kind of cultural amnesia that is misleading and dangerous. Eating is an agricultural act. Eating ends the annual drama of the food economy that begins with planting and birth. Most eaters, however, are no longer aware that this is true. They think of food as an agricultural product, perhaps, but they do not think of themselves as participants in agriculture. They think of themselves as consumers.

– Wendell Berry, Our Sustainable Table

From the outset of human history, the study of food has been a foundation of natural learning. For day-to-day survival, the first peoples conducted in-depth environmental explorations in search of edible roots, plants, nuts, seeds, and berries using their knowledge and experience of their immediate surroundings. By attuning to the land and rhythm of the seasons, they figured out not only where to harvest wild food, but also, where and how to store it for long winters. Food was indeed at the center of the earliest curriculum.

These early explorations of food have evolved into contemporary studies of nutrition, botany, herbology, agronomy, husbandry, domestic economy, chemistry, agriculture, and even minerology. Drawing from these primal studies of food, modern communities are re-learning humans' proper place in the environment and regaining the skills to gather, grow, and hunt food in a sustainable way.

With less than 2 percent of its population engaged in cultivating food, the United States is particularly in need of developing a comprehensive food studies curriculum for communities of learners. Because of rampant food illiteracy among children, California was the first state in the U.S. to begin the Garden in Every School Initiative that has been gaining momentum across the country. The time is ripe to initiate programs that focus on educating ourselves about what our food system looks like today and how to insure its long-term health.

How does a community start with food studies? In the words of Wendell Barry, a farmer, poet, and sustainable food systems advocate from Kentucky: "… only voluntarily, the same way that one went in—by restoring one's consciousness of what is involved in eating, by reclaiming responsibility for one's own part in the food economy."

The cornerstone to any activities and projects around food studies lies in Sir Albert Howard's illuminating principal that we should understand "the whole problem of health in soil, plant, animal, and man as one great subject." In other words, we begin by seeing ourselves as an integral part of the larger food web that ultimately encompasses each insect, blade of grass, and microorganism across the planet.

GETTING STARTED WITH NATURAL AND CULTURAL STUDIES

Tell me your landscape and I will tell you who you are.
– Dalia Pagani, *Mercy Road*

Human cultures naturally reflect the ecology of the region in which they develop. The food, housing, clothing, and culture of the indigenous peoples of the North American continent, for example, mirrored the unique watersheds of the regions in which they evolved—from the northern woodlands to the middle plains, the southwest deserts to the northwest coast. Out of this knowledge came a deep reverence for all living beings.

As an essential part of the ecology of a particular area—the climate, geography, etc.—humans' relationships with the land, and with one another, formed the

---

CASE STUDY: SANTE FE, NEW MEXICO

Santa Fe's Cooking with Kids

Providing children with opportunities to experience their own cultural heritage through food growing and food preparation is becoming a primary focus of learning in many regions. Adjacent to the school garden and beside the schoolyard orchard at E.J. Martinez Elementary School in Santa Fe, New Mexico, students bake bread and empañaditas, a traditional Spanish turnover stuffed with veggies and meat, in their own outdoor oven, or *horno*. Growing and preparing both traditional and non-traditional foods with children has been the mission of Santa Fe's Cooking With Kids program, begun by local restaurant owner and mother Lynn Walters. Inspired by the prospect of helping to teach Santa Fe's children to take control of their diets by making their own foods themselves, Walters has sold her restaurant to assist the Santa Fe public school system to  shift its school lunch programs toward more locally grown and locally made foods in close partnership with the students and their families.

basis of their culture. Through the ages, the language of the land has been translated into the customs, folkways, music, dance, stories, idioms, and rituals of the people who have lived on that land.

The ancient ways of knowing and ways of being have formed a lasting legacy that still endures. These reservoirs of knowledge live on in all peoples who maintain an intimate connection to the land, such as farmers, hunters, horticulturalists, hikers, bikers, naturalists, and many more. Through archeology, art, history, music, song, visual and performing arts, anthropology, sociology, poetry, and literature, modern cultures endeavor to rediscover and give voice to the earth-based cultural traditions that offer great insights for inhabiting this unique place we call home.

The older stories in particular still hold a special power over our imaginations. Traditionally, it has been the elders who weaved the intricate tales and legends in which the animals and plants become the characters of moral teachings about the most righteous and reverent ways of honoring the life force in all creation. Today, the power of story to captivate children is as strong as ever, from bedtime stories and nursery rhymes, to show-and-tell circles and even contemporary films. The recent re-emergence of older, more holistic stories is testament to our yearning for authentic, time-honored narratives that will heal our perceived separation from nature.

These place-based stories that take us back to indigenous times are still readily available and can be looked to as a way of restoring a balance within ourselves, within our communities, and within the larger biotic world. By their re-telling, we can reorient ourselves to a specific place, and begin to find our own niche in the community's ecosystem. These ecological teaching tales are living evidence of the curriculum that the earth provides for every generation.

Key to any sustainable culture is incorporating into our stories, myths, written records, laws, and daily lives the practices and beliefs reflecting our natural ecology. In contemporary society, among the most difficult aspects of learning the centuries-old teachings of our ancestors is aligning indigenous ways of understanding the world with our own patterns of behavior that have been methodically refined over generations. Simply running a recycling project or collecting oral histories is not sufficient to change the deeply held values and beliefs that determine the way we act in the world.

These age-old ways of learning do not make good television and will not be featured in a blockbuster movie or video game anytime soon. An ecological education demands a deep and lasting commitment to the immediate environment, to fully live in and learn from a particular place. Indeed, moving deeper into this learning demands not that we perpetually grasp for a technologically advanced future, but rather that we remember the teachings of the earth that always have been here and always will be.

Dimension Three: Ecological Action

In the last four decades, the world population has more than doubled, world economic output has increased fivefold, and the same is predicted for the next 40 to 50 years. This unprecedented growth is altering the face of the earth and the composition of the atmosphere. Meeting needs now and in the future requires a major shift in the relationship of humans to the natural environment. This requires a "paradigm shift" in the thinking, values, and actions of all individuals and institutions worldwide, a shift that calls for a long-term societal effort to make environmental and sustainability concerns a central theme in all education.

– Anthony Cortese, Second Nature: Advancing Human and Environmental Well-being Through Learning

If a more ecologically responsive culture is to fully emerge and drive our economic, political, and social organizations, then people of every age and from all walks of life must continue the work of reconstructing those institutions. From homes to schools to the workplace, we face the daunting challenge of building a culture that reflects the basic ecological principles and cycles that have shaped humans since pre-history.

Living in a society that spends 95 percent of its time indoors, we must first simply open our doors and step outside to fully appreciate the immediate world around us. Just as our forebears actively engaged in the natural world in order to meet their basic human needs, so must we create opportunities that reconnect us with our immediate environment, our means of sustenance, and our fellow beings. Likewise, truly integrating ecological action into the learning process of children will require the commitment of educators to renew the learning process through direct experience with nature.

Study Project Ideas for Conducting Action Research in...

... the Local Watershed:

✔ Conduct a watershed-wide natural resource inventory.

  • map your entire watershed, from source to mouth; include tributaries.

  • identify all ecosystems and habitats that are formed by the watershed.

  • include woodlands, waterways, lakes, ponds, reservoirs, quarries, gravel pits, marshes, swamps, bogs, wetlands, ag land, parks, mountains, fisheries.

✔ Make a 4x8 foot relief map depicting all of the above features. Identify locations of towns, villages, and cities; as well as major industries and businesses, roadways, and housing developments.

✔ Describe how the watershed was formed geologically, and how it developed in the ways it has. Specify how particular geologic features formed in the way they did.

✔ Define the human settlements in this watershed over time, beginning with indigenous peoples, continuing with European explorers, colonial settlers, immigrant populations, present inhabitants.

✔ Develop a human impact statement: Identify how human activities impact and have impacted the local environment through industry, transportation, waste, housing, commercial activity, agriculture. Which would you consider extractive and harmful, and which are sustainable and beneficial?

Other study project ideas include activities centered on:

• botanical gardens.

• habitat trails.

• wildlife ecology: enhancement of habitat for beneficial birds and animals.

• all species inventoried and studied: keep an ongoing record for comparing and contrasting what's there now, and into the future.

• renewable energy systems design focusing on solar, thermal, geothermal, wind, wood.

• biological waste treatment systems.

• weekend and nightly workshops on any and all of the above.

• on-line information exchanges.

• data collection and monitoring compiled into a seasonal newsletter updating communities about the health of their ecosystems.

... the Local Culture:

✔ Visit the local historical society, libraries, and museums, and interview area anthropologists and indigenous educators. What has been the legacy of the various ethnic communities in your area to the local environment? What beliefs and practices still exist which subscribe to the New Golden Rule, page 126, that each generation meet its needs without jeopardizing the prospects of future generations to meet their own needs?

✔ Map out who's who and what's what in your community of living cultural resources: include specific people, places, and architecture, as well as artifacts and natural landmarks. Begin with the indigenous people of your area.

✔ Develop a plan to orient people to the cultural story of your community. Build a developmental continuum of educational activities for students of all ages to explore the local cultural history.

✔ Collect oral histories: Students and community members can interview and record stories of area elders and historians and document them using videos, tapes, big books.

✔ Share elders' stories, knowledge, and wisdom weekly through lunches, socials, or outings.

✔ Host intergenerational community events exchanging stories, life experiences, and information about the diverse cultural heritage of your community: include topics such as food traditions (gardening, meals, etc.); relationships to the land (farming, fishing, hunting); values and ethics (helping others, competition, community, individualization).

✔ Conduct a personal cultural beliefs and practices inventory: Record daily activities encoded in specific cultural traditions or habits (past or present) that are directly related to the natural environment: walking, driving, biking, smoking, recycling, eating fast food, composting, shopping, extended meals with family, camping, etc.

✔ List three local examples of cooperative cultural activity not induced by economic necessity.

... Local Food Growing:

• prototype demonstration of intensive home food systems

• small fruit and vegetable research gardens

• animal husbandry workshops

• edible landscapes that teach through signage and interactive displays

• demonstration of local grain production and processing

• outdoor bread oven

• intergenerational gardening activity units based on community historic theme gardens

• medicinal herb garden; ethnobotany workshops

• aquaculture as an integrated system

• home and community compost systems

• cooking and culinary arts

• food processing area for drying, freezing, canning

• nutrition center

• seed saving of heirloom and adaptable hearty varieties

• heirloom seed bank

• perennial permaculture plan

• food co-ops and buying clubs

• farmers' markets

• meals-on-wheels

• inspiration through arts, murals, drama, totems, painting, sculpture, music

• self-guided walking tour through community mosaic garden

The following action steps are arranged in a four-fold sequence: research, policy, service, and restoration. The educational process described here takes place primarily within the local community—in gardens, farms, orchards, markets, food shelves, soup kitchens, senior centers, historical societies, local libraries, work places, forests, meadows, and riversides.

SUSTAINABLE LIVING/LEARNING CENTERS (PUBLIC SCHOOLS)

Through a carefully honed participatory democratic process, voices of students would be heard alongside those of elders and the voices of the land to articulate a common vision for the long-term health and sustainability of the whole biotic community.

This process would entail local research into and demonstration of ecologically viable projects that focus on basic human life-support systems: food, water, energy, shelter, waste management, and culture.

The purpose of these living/learning centers would be to demonstrate how to cultivate more ecologically oriented lifestyles. The structure of the working day at such centers would no longer include the arbitrary 50-minute class period, but instead be oriented toward a much more open-ended and fluid schedule, providing learners ample time for in-depth learning experiences out in the world. The traditional classroom would be the place for writing up research findings in reports, creating newsletters and newspapers, preparing presentations, compiling surveys, planning outreach activities, and practicing the performing and fine arts.

Anyone could visit to conduct research or simply ask questions on a wide variety of topics related to the local ecology: insect pests, pernicious weeds, hardy small fruits for backyard growing, espalier fruit trees, fast hot compost systems, preserving, canning, freezing/drying local foods, soil testing, cover cropping, crop rotations, plantings for beneficial insect/bird/wildlife habitats, agro-forestry, macroinvertebrates and the health of local waterways, the carrying capacity of the local ecosystem, and so on.

Working alongside community members, the students would apply their findings to real-life local problems through such projects as conducting a community-wide needs assessment, developing a municipal food policy, and practicing ecologically sustainable land-use methods. Collaborative action research can also take place among centers in the same water-

Putting the Lessons of Nature to Work

"I learned that rainforests are more efficient, and more creative, than any business in the world."

– Tachi Kiuchi, managing director of Mitsubishi Electric Corp., after touring an equatorial rainforest

A growing number of cutting-edge global businesses are recognizing the efficiency of redesigning their workplace to follow ecological cycles and patterns. Ecological accounting systems, for example, are enabling companies to cut costs and boost environmental performance by identifying ways to provide more services using less energy, materials, land, or other resources.

Mitsubishi Electric Corporation, which Fortune Magazine has called one of the world's largest industrial and financial conglomerates, has adopted what is called the Natural Step Process, a set of principles embracing the notion that materials should not be produced at a faster rate than they can be broken down and integrated into existing cycles of nature.

Inspired by a working tour of an equatorial rainforest sponsored by the Rainforest Action Network, the managing director of Mitsubishi Electric, Tachi Kiuchi, implemented this unique corporate management process for his company.

"Corporate executives must structure companies so that they are not structured like a machine—which cannot learn—but like a living organism, which can," Mr. Tuichi says.

In addition, Mitsubishi Electric has agreed to protect local Third World communities that rely on natural resources that are often depleted through industrial practices. The corporation has also made an unusual pledge to support indigenous communities, rooted in place, with adequate food, potable water, a clean environment, and "meaningful work." Randy Hayes, the Rainforest Action Network's Executive Director, said, "I see this agreement as a template," noting that other corporations that use the template will be assisting in "the transition to a more sustainable society."

Imagine an educational system which prepared young people for this kind of working environment!

shed, culminating in an annual watershed council and congress.

1. Research: Pre-service Ecological Education

All adult students studying to become teachers would be schooled in a curriculum rooted in the principles of ecology, guided by the New Golden Rule—that each generation meet its needs without jeopardizing the prospects of future generations to meet their own needs.

As part of their integrated classroom preparation, teachers would formulate the foundations for the ecological theory, content, methods, and assessments that meet the needs of students in finding their own unique niche in their local watershed. Student teachers could choose a specific human settlement in their community's history, for example, and develop inquiry-based, seasonal curriculum units around the food and agricultural practices, the economy, and the culture of the people during that time period. The recreation of arts, music, dance, and song that made up the cultural fabric of the historic community would be incorporated into the curriculum units. Student teaching would be done at the sustainable living/learning centers in conjunction with each center's specific food and ecological long-term education plan.

2. Policy: A Foodprint for Local and Regional Food Security

A local food policy is a systematic plan to provide everyone in a given locality a diet of at least 2,000 calories per day of safe, healthy, affordable, and nutritious food that is grown as close to home as possible. The goal of a food policy is to insure food security for all, so that an entire community is able to feed itself and minimize its impact on local and global natural resources. Creating a food policy involves researching and documenting the overall food needs in the community, mapping all existing and available land for growing food to meet those needs, implementing workable strategies for growing and marketing food locally, and enacting a strategic plan for educating the community about food and nutrition across generations, ensuring that everyone knows how to grow and prepare their own food. Creating and implementing a local food policy is just one measure a living/learn-

ing center could undertake as part of its emergent curriculum.

Seven Basic Steps for Creating a Local Food Policy:

1. Define the geographic boundaries of your community. Collect data on total population, total food imports, food grown and consumed locally, local foods exported.
2. Identify and map areas where food could be grown locally: community gardens, rooftops, city parks, vacant lots.
3. Research and create a plan for marketing locally grown food.
4. Identify possible food processing centers: canning, drying, storage, freezing. Detail local entrepreneurial and economic opportunities.
5. Hold community forums to plan local food growing and to cultivate appreciation for and understanding of the advantages of locally grown food.
6. Develop a multi-year strategic "food-shed plan."
7. Develop an educational plan for local food studies focusing on nutrition, service, entrepreneurship.

3. Service: Fostering Community Connections

A fundamental principle of sustainable living/learning centers is that everyone's basic needs in the community should be met regardless of their ability to produce or pay. This commitment would be fostered throughout every project and area of ecological study, so that it would become second nature for students to apply what they learn toward making their community a better place to live. Thus, service learning becomes not simply an add-on, but an essential part of a school day in which the students are connected to everything that they study.

Community Service Learning Project Ideas

- community newspaper or newsletter, featuring positive news stories, in-depth historical articles, ecological updates (bird migrations, restoration areas), habitat puzzles, garden tips, recipes
- weekly community meals and talent shows
- meals on wheels delivering youth-made meals to elders and shut-ins (delivered by a solar-powered car designed by students in school-to-work projects!)

- programs covering a wide range of environmental issues on community access TV, including topics like basic gardening, managing a home compost system, community news, watershed reports, preserving food
- volunteering at a food shelf or soup kitchen
- youth service corps: students build kitchen gardens, container gardens, compost systems, food-preservation facilities
- kids read and tell stories to elders
- municipal park maintenance and management: clean-up, raking and composting leaves, maintaining trails, mulching, signage, upkeep
- community beautification: planting and maintaining perennial flower beds, developing a local floral plan
- community foodscaping: small fruits, berries, edible flowers
- wildlife tracking resource center with tours and trips to identify wild edibles, wild plants, wildlife

4. Restoration:
Commitment to Place

One of the key problems in American society now … is people's lack of commitment to any given place. … The reconstruction of a people and of a life in the United States depends in part on people, neighborhood by neighborhood, county by county, deciding to stick it out and make it work where they are, rather than flee.

– Gary Snyder

Flowing out of awareness and knowledge of one's own watershed is the deep understanding of what constitutes a healthy and interdependent ecosystem. Based on this knowledge, students can become engaged in the restoration of area habitats using local tools and native plants, and working alongside naturalists, foresters, botanists, environmental engineers, and other professionals.

Groups can begin by studying, researching, and mapping local ecosystems and habitats as a foundation for building lifelong relationships with the hills, valleys, brooks, glens, and plains of the immediate environment. Growing out of the first-hand experience and understanding of the principles of ecology in the everyday natural world, teams next could develop a research plan to determine the health and sustainability of their local watershed. From this watershed research process, an ecosystem restoration plan can be developed, prioritizing the areas of greatest need.

Start-up questions to begin the process include: Which habitats are most unstable or suffer from the greatest erosion? What threatened, endangered, or rare species can be identified and protected? What specific habitats, food sources, and corridors do local species need to survive and thrive as they migrate from one region to another? What green belts should be conserved for sustainable economic activity such as agro-forestry with beneficial wildlife habitats?

Restoration Project Ideas

- Conduct riparian zone restoration projects: a long-term improvement plan along rivers and waterways that includes planting water-tolerant cultivars of shrubbery and plants to prevent erosion and benefit birds and wildlife.
- Create a habitat restoration nursery consisting of erosion controling plants, shrubs, and trees.
- Build birdhouses, birdfeeders, bat houses. Set them up in backyards and public buildings throughout the community to encourage greater diversity of birds, wildlife and insect eaters.
- Plant hummingbird gardens.
- Develop beneficial wildlife habitat landscapes, like shrubs with berries and seeds. Habitats include the four critical components for all animals to live: food, water, a place for safety, a place to raise young.
- Start an edible nursery of small fruits, berries, herbs (medicinal and culinary), dwarf fruit trees, nut trees, all from local root stock to fit your climactic zone.
- Institute a certification program for watershed conservationists—with clear benchmarks signifying attainment of the skills, knowledge, and values for restoring and maintaining the local watershed.
- Create public places for restoring our own relationship to nature such as healing gardens—natural places for quiet reflection and regeneration to reconnect.

Integrating the New and the Old: Returning to the Wisdom of the Land in Oaxaca

– by Gustavo Teran, U.S.-Mexico Cultural Exchange Facilitator

In the face of serious ecological degradation and deepening social and economic problems, many rural communities in Oaxaca, Mexico are rediscovering workable strategies for developing their local economy that are rooted in their own history and natural environment. By reinvigorating their traditional value system and kinship networks, they are, as Oaxacan community educator Gustavo Esteva puts it, "regenerating the art of living and dying."

In "soil cultures" like this San Felipe community, the production, preparation, and consumption of local food is an integral part of virtually every aspect of community life. Social relationships, family and community gatherings, ecological health, and economic sustainability are all related to the production of food.

Coffee plantations clearly have disrupted this pattern because, even though coffee brings in badly needed cash, it transforms a highly diversified and well-integrated subsistence farming system into an export-oriented monoculture. In a volatile world market of wildly fluctuating coffee prices, however, many Oaxacan communities are interplanting within the rows of the old Spanish coffee plantations their traditional crops of beans and corn. This way, they are able to maintain their link to the global market by continuing to grow coffee, but in a more limited way that allows them to provide for their basic food needs.

Communities in Oaxaca have also organized to educate children about sustainable forest practices including tree-planting field trips in depleted forests, hands-on participation in small-scale lumber enterprises, and workshops on interdependence within the forest ecosystem. Interestingly, these are all led by volunteer community groups because many schools are still resistant to changes in their conventional curriculum.

Visualize a future in which schools open their doors to the kinds of practical learning activities that communities in Oaxaca are organizing in order to restore their connection to their own natural heritage.

Dimension Four: Ecological Consciousness

We are ... highly evolved deep air animals. We are of the earth; our flesh is grass. We live in the cycle of birth and death, growth and decay. Our bodies respond to daily rhythms of light and darkness, to the tug of the moon, and to the change of seasons. The salt content of our blood, our genetic similarity to other life forms, and our behavior at every turn, give us away. We are shot through with wildness. Call it biophilia, or the ecological unconscious, the earth is inscribed in us, we are of the earth. We have an affinity for nature. What do we do about that simple but overwhelming fact?

– David Orr, *Earth in Mind*

Clouds gather above, a wind kicks up, the air is charged with the scent of rain. Suddenly, a bolt from the sky shatters the silence and a single raindrop streaks down your forehead. Look skyward, and taste the drops of water that dance down your cheeks.

The cycles that manifest outside appear inside as well. Consider that these very same water molecules entering your system to replenish your body have been recycled on the planet countless times over millions of years. And now, at this very moment, they are part of you.

How is it that the tiny drops of rain that fall from the sky continually recycle themselves season after season, trickling through the soil, swelling brooks and rivers, emptying into oceans, and evaporating to form clouds once more which continue the cycle around and around, generation after generation, in every region of the earth? How do we better synchronize our lives—our communities, our schools, our economy, our agriculture, our industry—that flow seemlessly with these natural cycles?

The backyard vegetable patch; the isolated fourth-grade garden science project at the local school; the once-a-year community green-up day; the Christmas food drive; the annual Arbor Day tree planting; the individual family farm. Together, these raindrops can sustain an ecological education and ways of living; separately they hit the ground, make a small impact, then quickly evaporate.

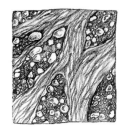

What happens when these drops of rain become numerous enough to begin merging?

As the rain picks up, small rivulets take shape, water starts to flow, there's movement: Like isolated raindrops joining together to form a more unified force, individual garden activities become seasonal integrated instructional units; students conduct a habitat inventory of their schoolgrounds and map out an educational nature trail; monitoring and data collection on the diversity and health of local species is begun; home compost systems develop from backyard gardens; neighborhood community gardens are organized; small farmers markets are formed.

What becomes of these thousands of tiny rivulets as they gather force?

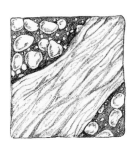

The thousands of rivulets are pulled down a hillside into small nooks, cavities, and hollows to form a muddy brook, gaining momentum: Just as a brook is formed by a network of tiny interconnected arteries, modest garden curricula developed in separate schools grow to become a district-wide focus on food and ecological studies, perhaps culminating in a five-year in-service professional development institute for all district teachers; through this institute, each school could develop an action plan for a historic theme garden and schoolyard habitat in every grade (see Chapter 9), including a student-produced garden/habitat newsletter and an electronic community bulletin board to share questions, ideas, and information with one another; intergenerational plantings of small fruit trees and berry bushes are initiated in local parks and homes; initial forums are held on developing a local food policy aimed at revitalizing local agriculture based on healthy ecosystems, with one primary goal that 50 percent of the food in the school cafeteria is grown locally; schools research and experiment with area edibles, herbs, medicinals, and rare and endangered plants, as well as the beneficial habitats for these species; innovative compost meth-

ods are experimented with to develop a local model for a sustainable food system; the community-at-large decides to research and develop entrepreneurial opportunities by incubating food and environmental local businesses through primary and high schools, colleges, technical schools, and local businesses.

What happens as the rain continues and the swelling brook winds its way down the hillside?

The brook flows into a determined river which draws all of the rushing waters from the surrounding basin as it races along the sloping valley floor: Like the granaries that sprung up around early America's rivers, pre-service teacher education programs blossom with a bioregional focus on watersheds, food and agricultural systems—along with local natural and cultural history—as part of a watershed academy; a regional plan for food security is implemented by communities within the same watershed, insuring all citizens a balanced, nutritious diet of locally grown food; out of this food policy, a regional economic system develops, focused on strengthening local businesses, sustainable land use management, and restoring and preserving the natural environment as the foundation for long-term economic development; model regional businesses have developed waste-free processes based on simple ecological methods that mimic natural ecosystems; the education system's sustainable living and learning centers have totally adopted the principles of ecology, developing curriculum theory, content, and methods patterned after the local ecology; young and old alike are engaged in finding real-work niches that fit into the web of the cultural ecosystem.

What happens with all of this power gathered from the watershed which has strengthened the river on its rugged journey?

By now the wild and forceful river has found its way to a magnificent coastal bay and is engulfed by the sublime enormity of the boundless ocean. At that moment along the same coastline, a wild diversity of once-sovereign rivers are likewise returning home to the primal sea. The sun shines strong over the turbulent ocean waters, drawing up water molecules to form billowing clouds that are driven back over land by the wind, gradually gathering the weight of accumulated moisture until the cloud bursts, and a drop of rain falls back to the earth.

When the river reaches the ocean, it quickly becomes clear that the whole is far, far greater than the sum of its parts. Likewise, the seemingly endless activities, project ideas, and program initiatives identified here are but mere drops of water in the ocean of human potential. Certainly, there are a multitude of national and global initiatives that should be undertaken to insure food and ecological security for all: food and ecology cultural exchange programs; electronic bulletin boards set up between communities around the world, sharing strategies, research, and units of study on living sustainably; a people's summit on maintaining the health and vitality of the earth's life support systems; a global biodiversity declaration of interdependence.

But the limitless possibility that oceans present and represent in the human imagination goes much deeper than merely networking what already exists on the earth's surface. Mythologically, oceans have borne the beginnings of life and the origins of our biotic memory.

So we return anew to the wellspring of consciousness itself where all things are possible, to those places where we can remember ourselves by becoming fully integrated into the earth's cycles that we are here imagining. As a species, we hold the potential to transform our human consciousness by reconnecting to

those first stories and lessons of our ancestors drawn from the wisdom of the earth.

Today we stand at the threshold of the next chapter of this age-old story, as communities across the land—from rural townships to seacoast cities, from suburban neighborhoods to city parks, from the prairie lands to the mountaintops—commit themselves to resettling their own watersheds by revitalizing regional agriculture, restoring local ecosystems, and reconstructing their own unique stories of the land.

It is the seeds of this ecological story that are first planted and nurtured in the child's garden. And as every child knows, anything we can imagine we can create.

Remembering and envisioning a time
when the children are all healthy
and the schools are life itself
when the gardens are abundant
and the farms are many
the streets are clean and food is plenty
the streams are clear and the forests strong
and the oceans are pure and bounteous
as our minds.

DESIGNING THE GARDEN SITE

(for Chapter Four, pages 32 and 34)

A. Creating a Base Map

Step 1: A simple way to measure distances is to pace them out. To do this, you must first measure and record the length of your regular walking stride. Start with feet together, take a normal walking step with your left foot, then your right; bring your feet together. This equals one pace. Measure this, and you are ready to go.) *Important note:* Boundaries can also be measured using a standard tape measure.

Step 2: Measure the total length of the boundary by counting the number of paces you walked from one end to the other, then multiply the number of paces by the length of one pace. Example: A fence along one edge of the property is 48 paces long, and each pace is five feet. The approximate length of the boundary fence is 240 feet. Record on a large piece of paper.

Step 3: Create a map scale by dividing the actual length of the boundary by the length of boundary line drawn on the paper. Example: The fence is 240 feet and the line drawn on the paper is twelve inches. 240 divided by 12 equals 20. Therefore the scale is 240':12", or 240':1'. Twenty feet on the school grounds would equal one inch on the base map. This can also be calculated using an architect's ruler.

Step 4: From the end point of the boundary just measured, pace the next boundary of the property. Record on the base map, estimating the degree of angle changes from one boundary to another.

Step 5: Repeat Step 4 until all the site's boundaries are recorded. Be sure to identify both the lengths and the types of boundaries drawn (fence, sidewalk, tree line, etc.). Where it is impossible to walk the boundary, estimate the distance and record.

Step 6: Standing at a significant junction of boundaries, use a compass to mark the direction of magnetic north. Record this on your base map.

B. Site Analysis

As you walk the school grounds, record the location of the following natural (functional) and human-made (utilitarian) elements in relation to the boundaries. Be sure to create symbols to identify any of these elements on your map, and make a map key explaining what each symbol represents. For example: Wavy lines indicate shrubs.

In addition, you may wish to jot down certain physical characteristics and personal impressions in the spaces below.

FUNCTIONAL ANALYSIS
Natural Elements

- Vegetation (inventory of trees, shrubs, grasses, flowers)
- Geology (rocks)
- Soils (soil tests, evidence of herbicide use?)
- Hydrology (wet areas, streams, puddles, indicator plants of wet areas include ferns, cattails, sedge)
- Birds and wildlife (including signs of tracks, scat, habitats)
- Insects (beneficial, pests, habitats)
- Solar (shade, dry areas)
- Winds (prevailing Westerlies)
- Slopes
- Sounds
- Additional observations

UTILITARIAN ANALYSIS
Human Relationships and Behavioral Patterns

- Buildings
- Parking areas (including roads)
- Sidewalks and pathways
- Playgrounds
- Playing fields
- Gardens
- Monuments
- Signs
- Drains and Sewers
- Water sources (spigots)
- Potential problems: herbicides, pesticides, pollution

- Other variables (fire hydrants, lampposts, trash containers, traffic)
- Internal boundaries (fences, etc.)
- Views (describe from north, south, east, west—list unique vistas)
- Circulation (student movement on the landscape—beyond sidewalks)

OTHER FACTORS TO LOOK FOR

- Wildlife habitat areas (piles of brush and cover, etc.)
- Shady areas for outdoor observation stations
- Edge habitats
- Signs of existing bird and wildlife.
- Possible problem areas (erosion, wet areas, poor drainage, heavy foot traffic)

C. Preliminary Site Design

These steps will assist you in brainstorming possible garden plans by helping you to see what already exists and to visualize how your garden might fit into the landscape. The preliminary site design process is also helpful for identifying open areas, edges, and multi-use niches for educational learning.

Step 1: Begin with a group discussion of ideas based on the needs assessment of your students, families, school, and community. Consider ecological and agricultural research areas, multi-use areas, artistic spaces, wild areas, areas for beneficial habitats, play spaces, etc.

Step 2: Place a piece of tracing paper over the base map. Using a pencil, make a preliminary circle (bubble drawing) over some areas you may want to include in the garden. For example, a Three Sisters Garden is excellent for learning about the first peoples of an area, so make a circle on your tracing paper to show where it could be located and label it. Do this for Historic Theme Gardens, Schoolyard Habitat Research areas, tool shed, wigwam, weather station, bird blind, water discovery pond, meadow-thicket habitat, forest, community gathering area, and other multi-use spaces. You can always revise your bubble drawings by removing the tracing paper, posting it as a reference, then laying a fresh piece of tracing paper over the base map to try out an alternative design. Rework design ideas until you find a plan that the group agrees will best serve the needs of your garden program. You may want to consult other community members to add any suggestions or ideas.

Important note: Remember to always remain flexible during the design process. Many things will change as you begin to implement the actual garden landscape design.

Step 3: On paper, link up the proposed garden-use areas with a circulation loop (walkways, pathways) to see the relationships of the elements on the site and how people will move from one area to the next. You may also want to consider arbors or hedges to delineate one area from the next. If you decide to recreate the story of your community by using Historic Theme Gardens, consider using clear boundaries between each area.

Step 4: Step back and take a good, long look at the preliminary site design. Is it too cluttered? Does it tell a story? Does it provide for all members of your community to be included (elders, handicapped people, toddlers)? Does it blend landscape design with educational opportunities? Are there plenty of spaces for people to sit, relax, observe, and simply enjoy the beauty of this place?

√   Are the walkways wide enough and do they connect all areas of the landscape?

√   Is compost located near the gardens?

√   Is the outdoor bulletin board centrally located?

√   Are there creative places and hidden secret spaces?

√   Is the design inviting? Does it make you want to participate?

Step 5: After you have answered the above questions, make any changes to the design that will best address the immediate needs of all participants.

D. Master Plan

To create a final master design of the garden, the group has a few options:

•   at a meeting, they can make suggestions, which the facilitator sketches on tracing paper to create small "bubble drawings" over the base map;

•   each member of the group can draw out his or her design separately on tracing paper, then everyone's design is brought before the whole group for consideration;

•   one person or a small team of people can be given the responsibility of creating a master garden map to present to the group.

Whichever option is chosen, the purpose of this final step of the design process is to have as many wild and creative design ideas as possible percolating to the surface, and then adapt those ideas to fit the natural and human-made features already extant at the site. As a general rule, a productive, friendly garden for children will have plenty of wide walkways, a spacious play area (where possible), and a courtyard with room for role-playing and theater.

The garden can be planned as one large vegetable plot to be tilled collectively, or there can be several smaller theme gardens surrounding a central common garden.

After you have received sufficient input, suggestions, and creative ideas, it is time to finalize the design. At this stage, you may want to consider seeking the assistance of a landscape architect or landscape designer. They may also be called in to help the design team and create a professional look and even build a model of the site for all of the community to see.

When the Master Plan is completed, it is time to detail all of the materials, quantities, and costs in order to create a budget. This is essential for making a realistic estimate of what is possible to do at what time. You may decide to host a huge spring community work day to build and install all the gardens and plant the orchards and perennials for the Schoolyard Habitat Research areas. The following year you may want to construct a Discovery Pond and begin to build Outdoor Habitat Research Classrooms. In ensuing years, the group may decide to install season extenders, a greenhouse, an arboretum, and so on.

The Master Plan will likely need a narrative description that explains the needs assessment, the design process, the recreational and educational objectives, the budget, and the time line for implementation. This packet accompanied by the actual garden design will be helpful as you go out into the community to seek in-kind and financial support and make presentations to community groups. Your students will become your best salespeople as their interest and ownership motivates others.

√   Keep in mind that over time, much of the plan will change from what was initially envisioned. This is the magic of building community around the educational landscape design process.

√   Always return to the needs assessment that inspired this process.

√   Take time to record your deliberations and discoveries via video, photographs, interviews, drawings, journal entries.

√   Most importantly: Enjoy yourself.

HORTICULTURE BASICS

A. Germinating Mixture

There is a wide range of materials that can be used to start seeds, from plain vermiculite or mixtures of soilless media to various specially prepared soil mixes. Experimentation and experience will help you to identify which one works the best for your conditions.

A good germinating mix should have a fine, uniform texture, be well aerated, free of insects, disease organisms and weed seeds, fairly low in fertility, and capable of holding and moving moisture.

A sterile, disease-free and insect-free medium is particularly important when starting seeds indoors. A fungus, known as damping off disease, can kill off your seedlings overnight. Insect pests will have no natural predators to hold down their numbers in your classroom, home, or greenhouse. Weed seeds will germinate and rob your seedlings of essential moisture and compete for space.

A soilless mix is a good starting medium that can be purchased or homemade. To create your own soilless mix, use four quarts shredded spaghnum moss to four quarts vermiculite, then add one tablespoon of superphosphate and two tablespoons of ground limestone. Mix thoroughly.

Soilless mixes should be thoroughly moistened before using them. They are naturally low in nutrients, which is fine for germination, but your seedlings will require regular watering with a diluted fertilizer soon after they emerge.

Do not use garden soil by itself to start seedlings; it is not sterile and it is too heavy to allow good drainage. If you want to use garden soil, mix it with peat moss and vermiculite or perlite and sterilize the mixture. Put the slightly moistened mixture in a heat-resistant container and place in a 250-degree oven. Use a candy or meat thermometer to make sure the soil reaches 180 degrees for 30 minutes. This can be a smelly process, depending on your soil, and you won't be able to bake large quantities at a time.

B. Containers

There are almost as many types of containers available for starting seeds as there are seeds. Again, experimentation and experience will help you decide what works the best for you.

You can purchase or make trays or flats. If you are going to use flats, a convenient size is 12 to 18 inches long, 12 inches wide, and two inches deep. Flats should have spaces of about one-eighth of an inch between the boards on the bottom, or a series of holes to allow for drainage. Good quality flats will last for many years, so they are quite economical.

Plastic cell packs are light weight, readily available, reusable, washable, easy to store, and uniform in size. Because they can be used for years, the price is reasonable.

Clay pots can be used for starting seeds, but they are heavy and tend to dry out quickly. They are generally not the best choice for seedlings.

Many people use peat pellets and peat pots to start seeds. If you use these, you can plant your seedlings directly in the garden without removing them from their pots. The disadvantages of peat pots and pellets are that they can only be used once, and they tend to dry out quickly.

Milk jugs, yogurt cups, egg cartons, and foil pie pans can also be used as containers for starting seedlings. Drainage holes must be provided. The lack of uniformity in size might be a problem if you have limited space for starting seeds.

Another option for seed starting is the use of a soil blocker. This device creates individual blocks of soil mixture into which seeds are sown. Soil blockers are available for making half-inch, two-inch, and four-inch blocks. The advantages of a soil blocker is the ease at which you can transplant each individual plant, transplanting shock is reduced, and after the initial cost of the tool, you never have to buy additional containers.

C. Seeding, Watering, Temperature, and Light

When is the best time to start seeds? It depends on what you want to plant, the length of your growing season, and the date of the last frost.

Consider first, what plants can be seeded directly into the ground and what must be started indoors. For plants started indoors, determine the optimal time to start each plant. The backs of seed packets are an excellent source for this information. Other good sources include general gardening references such as: *Gardener's Desk Reference, Rodale's All-New Encyclopedia of Organic Gardening*, and *Just the Facts*.

The time for seeding inside will usually range from four to 12 weeks prior to transplanting: four weeks for cucumbers and cosmos, six weeks for tomatoes and marigolds, eight weeks for eggplant and peppers, 10 weeks for impatiens and snapdragons, 12 weeks or more for pansies and begonias. The number of weeks you allow for indoor growth is determined by the speed of germination, the rate of growth, and the conditions you can provide for the seedlings.

A common mistake is to sow the seeds too early, then attempt to slow the growth of the seedlings by providing poor light or improper temperatures. The result is usually tall, weak, spindly plants that will do poorly when transplanted outside.

Always count backwards from the date you plan to set things outside to determine the date for starting indoors. Tomatoes only need six weeks inside before setting out. For example, start tomatoes around April fifth to plant outside on May fifteenth.

When you have a list of plants to be grown indoors, select your containers and growing medium (soil). Fill containers to within three-quarters of an inch from the top with the pre-moistened soil. Press down on the soil gently to provide a level surface. Sowing in rows allows for good light and air movement, which helps prevent damping off disease. Also, seedlings planted in rows are easier to label and handle at transplanting time.

Sow the seeds on the surface of the soil, then cover them with a sprinkling of soil to the correct depth as specified on the back of the seed packet. Planting seeds too deep is a common mistake resulting in poor germination.

Label each variety so that you don't forget what you planted. Include the date of sowing on the label.

Once your seeds have been sowed and labeled, cover them with a sheet of plastic so they won't dry out. At this stage, the containers do not need to be in direct sunlight or even under fluorescent lights. Do place them where temperatures will be warm enough for germination to occur. If the soil dries out and you must water before germination occurs, mist with a fine spray.

Strong light is important to insure healthy plant growth. As soon as plants emerge from the soil, put them directly under grow lights, with the lights as close as possible to the plants. Windowsills do not receive enough sunlight to sustain healthy plants. If plants are getting weak and leggy, they are not receiving enough light. Make sure the lights are on for 14 to 16 hours a day. Raise the lights as the plants grow to keep the leaves from touching the bulbs. Seedlings usually grow best when day temperatures are 65 to 70 degrees and night temperatures are between 55 and 60.

The best way to water seedlings is to set the containers in a pan or tray of warm water. When the soil is saturated, pour off any excess. Water each day by adding only enough water to keep the soil wet. Consistent moisture is one of the keys to good germination and good seedling growth. Allowing the soil to dry out, and then soaking it, will inhibit germination and weaken or kill seedlings.

D. Thinning and Transplanting

Thinning and transplanting are two very important tasks that, if done properly, will insure healthy seedlings.

Thinning involves removing some plants from groups that are growing too close together. Thinning allows the remaining plants more room and better conditions for growth. Plants growing too close together will compete with one another for water and nutrients. If you do not thin them, plants will not be healthy and the quantity and quality of your harvest will suffer. Crowded plants are weak and are prime targets for disease and insect infestations. You should thin plants as soon as true leaves are developing and you notice too many plants crowded together.

If you would like to save the seedlings, thin by transplanting. If you don't have room for all of the transplants, then thin by removing the smaller or weaker-looking plants. Cut them off at the soil line with scissors, or pinch them off with your fingernails. You may pull out the unwanted plants with tweezers. Do this very carefully, because you do not want to disturb the roots of the remaining plants. Gently water after you thin. If you have thinned salad greens, you can eat the thinnings. Put unwanted thinnings in your compost pile.

Transplanting is the process of removing young plants from the containers in which they were started into larger containers or the garden. The larger containers will give the plants room to develop bigger and stronger root systems and top growth. Some plants do not transplant well, such as peas, beans, corn, and most root crops. Other plant varieties are not stunted in the least when transplanted. These include peppers, onions, tomatoes, salad greens, and cabbages. Cucumbers and squash are possible to transplant, but must be handled very gently, and should be started in plastic yogurt containers or the like.

You can start transplanting after a couple weeks of good, vigorous growth. If possible check the root development of the plant. When roots are starting to emerge out the bottom of the soil, it is time to transplant. Transplant into clean, sterilized containers. The container must have drainage holes and should be considerably larger than the one the plant is growing in. Fill the containers to within one inch of the top with moistened soilless mix. Make a hole in the soil deep and wide enough to accommodate the roots of the seedling.

To remove a seedling from its container, hold it by a seed leaf and gently coax it out of the soil using a pencil or potting label. Do not grasp the seedling by the stem. If the stem is damaged, circulation of water and minerals to the upper part of the plant is cut off, and the plant will die. If you have used plastic cell packs, a seedling can be removed by gently squeezing the pack at the bottom. Lower the seedling into the hole and gently spread out the roots as much as possible. Fill with potting mix and press it down. Make sure the seedling is not buried deeper than it was originally. (Tomatoes are an exception to this rule and can set more roots if they are buried up to the top growth.) After transplanting, water with a dilute fertilizer, such as fish emulsion or sea kelp. If necessary, repeat this process before setting your plants outside. When planting out in the garden, follow these same steps.

E. Hardening Off

Hardening off is the process of gradually exposing plants that are grown indoors to the outdoor conditions. Plants that are not hardened off will often die or suffer severe setbacks when exposed to the harsher environment found outside.

Hardening off should be started at least one week before planting in the garden. First, move the plants to a sheltered location, where there is little wind and filtered sunlight. Bring the plants inside at night or cover them with a floating row cover or cold frame. Increase the exposure to direct sunlight by a half-hour each day. Reduce watering and fertilizing, but do not allow plants to dry out.

The hardening off process may initially slow the plant's growth, but this eventually allows for an easier transition into the garden without the risk of shock. When transplanted, plants should receive plenty of water and an initial dose of liquid fertilizer, such as fish emulsion or compost tea.

GARDENING WITH CHILDREN: 12 RULES TO GROW BY

Regardless of whether a garden program is planned only for the summer months or is to span the entire school year, the same guidelines apply for planning organized, creative activities that stir the imagination of every child.

1. Balance Structure with Freedom.

Strike a dynamic balance between a clear, consistent structure of theme-based activities and unstructured time to allow the children to follow their own curiosity in the garden. Children thrive on structured daily activities and consistency. Consider starting each day with a story, a snack, and a garden activity. At the same time, storytelling, painting, dance, and theater are powerful catalysts that free kids from the day-to-day routine in a large group.

2. Develop a Needs-Based Program.

As discussed in Chapter Two, the diverse needs of the children in your area should determine the day-to-day garden program. These needs might include nutrition education, outdoor recreation, outlets for artistic expression, cooperative group interaction, and local entrepreneurial opportunities. The effectiveness of the program is directly tied to the extent to which it meets these needs.

3. Create a Community-Centered Curriculum.

If it takes a village to raise a child, it takes a community to grow a children's garden. Seek out elders and others from your area to share their many skills and talents, from building birdhouses and making pickles to painting the garden landscape and telling stories.

4. See the Garden as an Interconnected Ecosystem.

Each niche of a garden contains unlimited creative learning opportunities for children, ranging from the makeup of the soil to botany, plant identification, insects, compost, and birdlife.

5. Attune the Senses to Garden Ecology.

Before formal learning and growing activities begin, attune children's senses to the natural and human environment that already exists at the site (see Attunement Exercise, page 33). This gives children a safe and secure start in this new environment.

6. Follow Children's Questions.

Respond to kids' natural curiosity in the garden as they ask why, where, when, how, and who. The best activities and programs grow out of the needs, interests, and questions of the children themselves.

7. Respond to Each Child's Age-Appropriate Needs.

Be sure to offer children challenging activities appropriate to their ages and interests. Activities in soil explorations, for example, will be different for children under age six than for seven- to nine-year-olds.

8. Adapt to Multiple Learning Styles.

Because not everyone learns the same way, offer gardening activities that stimulate the many different intelligences in all of us—spatial, musical, kinesthetic, linguistic, logical/mathematical, inter- and intrapersonal skills.

9. Seize the Teachable Moment.

In a garden, as in any ecosystem, unplanned events happen that capture the attention of children. Be flexible, ready to follow the flow of the moment to explore the wonder of the unexpected. Take time to examine an interesting beetle that shows up on a lettuce plant. Stop to inspect the unusual weed or mutation in a flower.

10. Define the Child's Role in the Garden.

To develop a feeling of ownership and pride in the garden, children need to have specific responsibilities and clear roles in maintaining the garden ecosystem. Consider creating a revolving garden-care wheel of jobs that can be rotated so each child has a new task every week.

11. Instill a Sense of Accomplishment and Self-Worth.

Simply by allowing kids to care for living things, gardening promotes a natural sense of self-worth. With their own eyes, children can watch seeds grow that they planted with their own hands. A well-designed children's garden program includes ongoing opportunities for children to take pride in the fruits of their labors and share their discoveries with family and friends.

12. Include a Community-Service Component.

As a social activity, gardening connects children to the wider community in countless ways. By sharing the bounty of the harvest with others—family, elders, the local pantry and soup kitchen—children give back the gifts of nature that they have been cultivating in their garden.

BOOKS & PERIODICALS

A smattering of books we like on gardening and children. All of these are interesting and useful reading for adults working with children and plants. Grade level is noted at the end of many of the descriptions as a guideline.

Abraham, Doc & Kathy, **Growing Plants from Seed**. 1991. Lyons & Burford Publishers. A complete how-to book for growing a wide variety of plants from seed. Older students, adult reference book.

Allardice, Pamela. Illustrated by Sue Ninham. **A–Z of Companion Planting**. Reprinted 1996, Harper Collins Publishers Limited. A blend of traditional wisdom and the latest scientific findings, all in a beautifully illustrated, easy-to-use, alphabetical guide.

Amon, Aline, **The Earth Is Sore**. 1981. Atheneum, NY, NY. A collection of Native American poems about nature and relationships. Very moving. For everyone.

Appel, G. and R. Jaffe, **The Growing Classroom: Garden Based Science.** 1990. Addison-Wesley Publishing Co., Menlo Park, CA. Developed by the Life Lab Science Program, Inc., *The Growing Classroom* is a guide for science teachers incorporating gardening as a focus theme for their classes. Interspersed with case studies, it shows how to cultivate team work using problem solving and communication skills and to teach earth science, plant propagation, interdependence, ecology, climate effects, and nutrition. Filled with activities and experiments with a strong scientific base.

Ault, R. et al., **Kids Are Natural Cooks: Child-tested Recipes for Home and School Using Natural Foods**. 1972. The Parents' Nursery School, Cambridge, MA in cooperation with Houghton Mifflin Co., Boston, MA. "Presents a variety of simple recipes based on natural foods with information on nutrition and basic cooking techniques." –Library of Congress

Bagust, Harold, **The Gardener's Dictionary of Horticultural Terms**. 1992. Cassell Publishers, London. Distributed in U. S. by Sterling Publ. Co., NY, NY. Reference.

Benjamin, Joan and Barbara W. Ellis, editors. **Rodale's No-Fail Flower Garden**. 1994. Rodale Press, Inc. Emmaus, PA. One book that explains how to plan, plant, and grow a beautiful flower garden. Excellent tips, many designs for flower gardens, and a nice guide of easy to grow flowers. Reference text.

Better Homes and Gardens, **Flower Gardening: Annuals, The Gardener's Collection**. 1993. Better Homes and Gardens Books.

Better Homes and Gardens, **Step-by-Step Successful Gardening: Annuals**. 1994. Better Homes and Gardens Books.

Bosse, Malcolm J., **The 79 Squares**. 1979. Thomas Y. Crowell, NY, NY. A 14 year-old boy on the edge of trouble, an old man with a dark past, and a garden make for an unlikely trio in this novel about friendship and finding oneself. Excellent reading. Full of wisdom and beauty. Grades 6–8.

Bourgeois, Paulette, **The Amazing Potato Book**. Illustrations by Linda Hendry. 1991. Addison-Wesley Publ. Co. Inc. Just about everything you have ever wanted to know about potatoes. History, experiments, recipes, games, facts, and fiction. Very readable and useful in the classroom. Fun for everyone

Bradley, Fern Marshall, **Rodale's All-New Encyclopedia of Organic Gardening**. 1992. Rodale Press. An excellent reference text to keep handy. The dictionary format makes it very easy to use. Students in grades 4 and up can use it as well as adults.

Bradley, Fern Marshall, **Rodale's Garden Answers, Vegetables, Fruits and Herbs**. 1995. Rodale Press. This book goes into detail about specific problems and questions. Keep it nearby just in case you need to know what is wrong with your tomatoes. Grades 4 and up, adults.

Brenner, Barbara, **The Earth Is Painted Green.** 1994. Scholastic Books. Poems that celebrate our planet through the seasons. All ages.

Buchanan, Carol, **Brother Crow, Sister Corn**. 1997. Ten Speed Press, Berkeley, CA. An exploration of early American Indians' centuries-old gardening traditions. A beautiful collection of Native songs and stories that offers a fresh perspective on our collective gardening history.

Buchanan, Rita, **A Dyer's Garden: From Plant to Pot, Growing Dyes for Natural Fibers**. 1995. Interweave Press, Inc., Loveland, CO. For anyone interested in growing the plants to use for dyeing fibers, this is an invaluable book. It takes you through garden design, planting, harvesting, and into the dye pot. Beautiful color photos illustrate the colors created by each plant on different natural fibers.

Budlong, Ware T. Illustrated by Grambs Miller. **Performing Plants**. 1969. Simon & Schuster, Inc., Children's Book Division, NY, NY. A fun and fascinating book that looks at the unusual and little-known aspects of a variety of plants. Learn how to grow a botanical clock or find out where north is using a plant. Ideas, experiments, and fun information. Middle school and up.

Burnie, David, **Dictionary of Nature.** 1994. Dorling Kindersley, NY, NY. Grades 3 and up.

Burnie, David, **Eyewitness Books: Plant.** 1989. Alfred A. Knopf, NY, NY. Younger students will love the wonderful color photographs. Good text for beginners to use to develop an understanding of plants.

Caduto, Michael and Joseph Bruchac, **Keepers of Life: Discovering Plants Through Native American Stories and Earth Activities for Children**. 1994. Fulcrum Publishing, Golden, CO. "*Keepers of Life* is a seed waiting to be planted. [You] provide the soil, water, sunlight and caring that enable the seed to sprout and bloom and the moments of discovery, excitement, and sharing that bring the stories and lessons to life." –from the Introduction.

Capon, Brian, **Botany for Gardeners**. 1990. Timber Press. A book for high school students or adults who want to know more botany.

Center for Sustainable Agriculture, **From A–Z in Sustainable Agriculture: A Curriculum Directory for Grades K–12**. The University of Vermont, Center for Sustainable Agriculture, Division of Agriculture, Natural Resources and Extension, Burlington, VT. Offers resources and contacts for educating youth about sustainable agriculture, food and fiber systems, and natural resources and their connections to our communities. Includes lists of texts, film, video, and equipment sources, as well as farms, educational centers and other crucial resources.

Coombes, Allen J., **Dictionary of Plant Names**. 1994. Timber Press. Information about the botanical names of over 1,000 plants. Gives a pronunciation guide, the country of origin, and meaning. Grades 5 and up, adult.

Cooney, Barbara, **Miss Rumphius**. 1982. Puffin Books. Most of us are familiar with this beautifully told and illustrated story of the "Lupine Lady." All ages.

DK Direct Limited, editors, **What's Inside? Insects**. 1992. Dorling Kindersley, Inc. NY. "A book designed to help young children understand the fascinating secrets of insects' bodies." Enlarged color photos of insects plus cutaway diagrams to reveal the inner workings of the insects. Created for younger children, but older children will also enjoy this unique book.

Dowden, Anne Ophelia, **The Clover & the Bee, A Book of Pollination**. 1990. HarperCollins Publishers. Describes in clear text and illustrates with beautiful full-color paintings and black-and-white drawings, the interrelationships between plants and animals. Grades 6–8 and older.

Dowden, Anne Ophelia, illustrated by the author. **From Flower to Fruit**. 1994. Ticknor & Fields Books for Young Readers, NY, NY. Details of flowers, fertilization, and seeds in clear, easy to understand text. Excellent botanical illustrations. Grades 5–8.

Dowden, Anne Ophelia. Illustrated by the author. **Look at a Flower**. 1963. Thomas Y. Crowell Co., NY, NY. This is a good book to use as a foundation

for serious botanical study. Excellent, clear explanations of classification, flower structure, pollination, and seed production. Meticulous illustrations. Description of 10 common plant families. Grades 6 and up.

Dowden, Anne Ophelia, illustrated by the author. **This Noble Harvest, A Chronicle of Herbs**. 1979. William Collins Publishers, Inc., Cleveland and New York. Interesting history of some common and not-so-common herbs. Excellent watercolor illustrations by the author. Will appeal to those who enjoy learning more about how people have used plants in the past. Grades 6 and up. **Note:** Some of Anne Dowden's books are no longer in print but are worth looking for in libraries.

Drees, M. et al, **Sembrar y Crecer: An Activity Guide for Gardening/ Nutrition in the Elementary School**. 1987. Meals for Millions/Freedom from Hunger Foundation. A teaching guide for elementary teachers, including daily lesson plans, and integrated curriculum activities for growing a garden and learning about nutrition. Includes experiments, recipes, and additional resources.

Eames-Sheavly, Marcia, **The Great American Peanut**. 1994. Cornell Cooperative Extension Publication. History, activities, recipes all centered around this important food crop. Grades 3–8 and adults.

Eames-Sheavly, Marcia and Tracy Farrell, **The Humble Potato, Underground Gold**. 1995. Cornell Cooperative Extension Publication. Entertaining stories, hands-on activities, and a botanical history of this food crop that has had a tremendous impact on so many cultures. Grades 3–8 and adults.

Eames-Sheavly, Marcia, **The Three Sisters**. 1993. Cornell Cooperative Extension Publication. History, scientific information, activities, recipes. Grades 3–8 and adults.

Fenton, Carroll Lane and Herminie B. Kitchen. **Plants We Live On: The Story of Grains and Vegetables**. 1971. The John Day Co., NY, NY. This book tells about food crops that were grown thousands of years ago and traces the travels of these plants. Covers plants from artichokes to zucchini. Grades 5 and up.

Garden Way Publishing, editors, **The Big Book of Gardening Skills**. 1993. Storey Communication, Pownal, VT.

A how-to book with very useful basic information. A reference text, not activities. Grades 4 and up.

Garden Way Publishing, editors, **Just the Facts!** 1993. Storey Communication. This book is set up in an easy-to-use chart format. Annual flowers, herbs, and vegetables as well as perennials are covered. Easy to use reference. Grade 3 with some adult help.

Gilkeson, Linda, Pam Pierce and Miranda Smith, **Rodale's Pest & Disease Problem Solver**. 1996. Lansdowne Publishing Pty Ltd. Published in 1996 Rodale Press, Inc. An easy-to-use A to Z guide to pests and diseases. Covers vegetables, herbs, fruits, flowers, shrubs, trees, and lawns. Excellent photographs. Describes symptoms, causes, preventions, and organic solutions. Very thorough.

Giono, Jean, **The Man Who Planted Trees**. 1985. Chelsea Green Publishing Co. A positive affirmation and vision of what one individual can do to take care of and change the natural environment. Lovely wood engravings by Michael McCurdy. Read aloud for younger students, older students, and adults.

Godkin, Celia, **What about Ladybugs?** 1995. Sierra Club Books for Children. Picture story-book about the dangers of using chemicals to control insects in a garden. Suitable for young children and also older students.

Greene, Janet, Ruth Hertzberg and Beatrice Vaughan, **Putting Food By**. 1988. The Stephen Greene Press, Inc. Considered by many to be the authority on preserving foods.

Guy, Linda, Cathy Cromell and Lucy K. Bradley, **Success with School Gardens: How to Create a Learning Oasis in the Desert**. 1996. Arizona Master Gardener Press, Phoenix. A "must have" for anyone gardening with schoolchildren in very dry conditions, this book also has excellent appendices listing all sorts of resources, especially for southwestern growers.

Halpin, Anne, **Horticulture Gardener's Desk Reference**. 1996. Macmillan, NY. An indispensable reference desk. This one has quickly joined *Rodale's All-New Encyclopedia of Organic Gardening* to become a classic horticultural reference.

Hays, Wilma and R. Vernon. Illustrated by Tom O'Sullivan. **Foods the Indian Gave Us**. 1976. Ives Washburn, Inc., NY, NY. A fascinating history of the foods given to us by the indigenous peoples of the Americas. Also contains some basic gardening information and a cookbook. Grades 5 and up.

Hershey, David, **Plant Biology Science Projects.** 1995. John Wiley & Sons Inc. Twenty-one science experiments using plants. Middle school.

Hill, Lewis and Nancy, Bulbs, **Four Season of Beautiful Blooms.** 1994. Storey Communications. One of the best books currently available about using flowering bulbs.

Jacobs, Betty E. M., **Growing and Using Herbs Successfully.** 1981. Storey Communications. Tips for starting herbs indoors and outdoors, how to harvest and store herbs, cultural information for 64 herbs, plus marketing ideas.

James, Wilma Roberts, **Know Your Poisonous Plants.** 1989. Naturegraph Publishers. An extensive list of poisonous plants that includes information about what parts of the plant are poisonous as well as symptoms of poisoning. A list of poisonous plants is essential when working with children.

Johnson, Jinny, **BUGS: A Closer Look at the World's Tiny Creatures.** 1995. A Reader's Digest Kids Book, Marshall Editions Developments Ltd., NY and Montreal. Kids will love this book! The pictures are huge so details of the insects are clearly seen. Good text and pictures showing the insects in actual size. Grades K and up.

Jones, Pamela, **Just Weeds: History, Myths, and Uses.** 1994. Chapters Publishing. A useful book for exploring common "weeds."

Kite, L. Patricia, **Gardening Wizardry for Kids.** 1995. Barron's Educational Series, Hauppage, NY. The activities in this book are very basic, but the stories about the history of common foods will be enjoyed by both young and old. Grades K–5.

Lauber, Patricia. photographs by Jerome Wexler. **From Flower to Flower: Animals and Pollination**. 1986. Crown Publishers Inc., NY, NY. Fabulous close-up photos of flowers and insects at work. Clear text explains how flowers and the animals who pollinate them benefit each other and humans. Grades 5–8.

Lerner, Carol, **Dumb Cane and Daffodils.** 1990. Morrow Junior Books, NY, NY. An illustrated guide to the most common poisonous house and garden plants. Excellent color botanical drawings as well as pencil drawings illustrate the very readable text. Grades 5 and up.

Lerner, Carol, **Plant Families.** 1989. William Morrow & Co., NY, NY. A look at 12 of the largest and most common plant families. Good, clearly written information. Latin names are given for the families with a pronunciation key. Kids and adults will love the beautiful botanical drawings that show enlarged flower details. This author has written a number of other books about plants using a similar format. Grades 4 and up. Color drawings are suitable for all ages.

Life Lab Science Program, **Getting Started: A Guide for Creating School Gardens as Outdoor Classrooms**. 1997. Center for Ecoliteracy, Berkeley, CA. A very well-written guide with all of the basics for getting a school garden started, including special features of model school gardening programs around the country. Life Lab is one of the pioneering organizations in the modern school gardening movement (see page 83).

Loewer, Peter, **Rodale's Annual Garden.** 1988. Wings Books. Pictures and information about growing annual flowers. Reference. Grades 3–4.

Matthews, William H., **Soils.** 1970. Franklin Watts, Inc. A good primer on the subject. Grades 4 and up.

McDonald, Lucille. **Garden Sass: The Story of Vegetables.** 1971. Thomas Nelson Inc., Camden, NJ. Colorful stories about vegetables. Includes solid background information as well as myths. Grades 5 and up.

McRae, Bobbi A., **Colors from Nature: Growing, Collecting and Using Natural Dyes.** 1993. Storey Communications Inc., Pownal, VT. How to grow your own dye plants, materials you can use from the grocery store, how to recognize and collect wild plants, all described in easy-to-understand language. Information on processing dyes and instructions for over one dozen craft projects using naturally dyed materials.

Michalak, Patricia S. and Linda A. Gilkeson, Ph. D., **Rodale's Successful Organic Gardening: Controlling Pests and Diseases.** 1994. Rodale Press. A must-have book. Good color pictures of insects and common plant diseases. Provides information about the life cycles of insects, the best time to control them, and organic controls. Also has a section about beneficial insects. Adult level text; students grades 3 and up can use the pictures to begin to identify an insect or disease.

Mitchell, Barbara , **A Pocketful of Goobers: A Story About George Washington Carver.** 1986. Carolrhoda Books, Inc. Biography. Lots of interesting facts. Fun to read. Grades 3–5.

The National Gardening Association Dictionary of Horticulture. 1994. Penguin Books, NY, NY. A useful companion to Harold Bagust's The Gardener's Dictionary of Horticultural Terms, which is not easily available.

National Gardening Association, **Grow Lab: Activities for Growing Minds** and **Grow Lab: A Complete Guide to Gardening in the Classroom.** 1990. National Gardening Association. Activities for K–8, many extensions, ideas for creating learning units using plants, basic how-to plans for building your own Grow Lab, reproducible worksheets. An indispensable aid for gardening inside.

Neal, Bill, **Gardener's Latin.** 1992. Algonquin Books of Chapel Hill. Definitions, facts, myths. For students and adults who are curious about words.

Ocone, Lynn with Eve Pranis, **The National Gardening Association Guide to Kids' Gardening.** 1983. John Wiley and Sons, NY, NY. Information about developing gardens with and for kids, getting community involved, site designs, and activities. A guide for teachers, parents, and community members.

Pellowski, Anne, **Hidden Stories in Plants.** 1990. Macmillan Publ. Co., NY, NY. Easy-to-tell stories about plants from around the world. Creative activities. Grades K–8.

Pleasant, Barbara, **The Gardener's Weed Book.** 1994. Storey Communications. Useful guide to help identify weeds. Reference.

Powell, Eileen, **From Seed to Bloom: How to Grow Over 500 Annuals, Perennials and Herbs.** 1994. Storey Communications. This thorough guide can be used as a reference book by children in grades 3 and up.

Pringle, Laurence, **Being a Plant.** 1983. Thomas Y. Crowell Junior Books, NY, NY. Explores the life processes of plants as well as the complex interrelationships between plants and animals. Illustrations by Robin Brickman. Grades 6–8.

Project Roots, **Exploring Gardening Through Classroom Activities: Reaching Our Outdoors Through Science.** 1981. Lansing School District, Lansing, MI. A curriculum guide that offers detailed lesson plans, including activities, experiments, and assessment for gardening as an alternative science program. Very detailed, scientific, and teacher directed.

Rahel, E. et al., **The Garden Organizer: A Guide to Community Gardening in Cleveland.** 1986. The National Gardening Association, Burlington, VT. A step-by-step guide for organizing, planning, managing, and preserving urban community gardens. Written for the volunteers of community gardens in Cleveland, Ohio.

Rahn, Joan Elma, **Plants That Changed History,** 1982. Atheneum, NY, NY. Stories of five plants that have made a mark in history. An engaging book that underscores the importance of plants in our everyday lives. Illustrations. Grades 5–8.

Reader's Digest Illustrated Guide to Gardening. 1992. Reader's Digest Association, Pleasantville, NY. Reference text with a wealth of information about flowers, shrubs, trees, and vegetables, as well as plant disorders and weeds.

Readman, J., **Muck and Magic: Start Your Own Natural Garden with Colorful, Simple Projects.** 1993. Search Press, Ltd., Great Britain. Filled with simple activities for primary level students to begin exploring gardening from the ground up. Includes many projects and experiments for the classroom.

Riotte, Louise, **Carrots Love Tomatoes: Secrets of Companion Planting.** 1975. Storey Communications. If you are interested in companion planting, this is a good book to begin with.

Rubin, L., **Food First Curriculum: An Integrated Curriculum for Grade 6.** 1984. Institute for Food Development Policy, San Francisco, CA. This anti-hunger curriculum focuses on exploring the underlying issues of hunger and empowering students to take action locally. It looks at hunger as a global issue: where our food comes from, why people experience hunger, malnutrition, and starvation, who is hungry, and what we can do. Great stories and activities on nutrition, world geography, political science, and economics.

Salisbury, J., **The Green Classroom Program: A Teacher's Guide to a Garden-based Science Curriculum.** 1988. The New Alchemy Institute, East Falmouth, MA. A month-by-month, step-by-step guide to integrating gardening in the science class. Carefully tailored to meet the needs of the annual school calendar, *The Green Classroom Program* offers activities, hand-outs, diagrams, charts, and resources for every season.

Schneck, Marcus, **Creating a Hummingbird Garden.** 1995. Simon and Schuster. Includes what plants to grow and when they flower. Reference.

Schneck, Marcus, **Garden Bird Facts.** 1996. Barnes & Noble, Inc. Quarto Publishing. A beautifully illustrated book packed full of answers and facts. Photographs, charts, and diagrams make it very easy to identify North America's favorite birds. Information is provided about how to attract birds with feeders and plantings. Also includes information on bird behavior, evolution, coloration, and migration. An indispensable book for all ages.

Selsam, Millicent E., with photographs by Jerome Wexler. **Mimosa: The Sensitive Plant.** 1978. William Morrow and Company, NY, NY. An entire book devoted to this plant that is so loved by children. Great photos and explanations. Grades 3 and up.

Selsam, Millicent E., with photographs by Jerome Wexler, **Vegetables From Stems and Leaves.** 1972. William Morrow and Co., Inc., NY, NY. Examines 12 foods that come from stems and leaves. Good introduction to the foods we eat and how they relate to plants. Grades K–4.

Selsam, Millicent E., **Where Do They Go? Insects in Winter.** 1981. Scholastic Inc. Describes what happens to common insects in winter. Grades 2–4.

Skelsey, A., **Growing Up Green: Parents and Children Gardening Together.** 1973. Workman Publishing Co., NY, NY. A curriculum guidebook filled with activities, experiments, and observations designed to encourage a love of nature and an exploration of gardening. Includes recipes for the harvest and a code of ethics for exploring nature.

Starcher, Allison Mia, **Good Bugs for Your Garden.** 1995. Algonquin Books of Chapel Hill. A great book about beneficial insects, what they eat, and what plants attract them.

Stokes, Donald and Lillian and Ernest Williams, **The Butterfly Book.** 1991. Little, Brown & Co. Color photographs, information about different species and food preferences.

Storey Publishing Bulletins, Storey Communications, Pownal, VT. An assortment of bulletins on a large variety of topics. Inexpensive.

Thesman, Jean, **Nothing Grows Here**. 1994. HarperCollins Children's Books, NY, NY. A girl's struggle to come to terms with loss and changes, and how gardens and friendships help. Grades 5–8.

Tilgner, Linda, **Let's Grow.** 1988. Storey Communications. Seventy-two gardening adventures for children of all ages. Activities range from indoors to woodland walks. Each activity lists materials needed. Also has a section with activities by seasons.

Tounge, P., **The Good Green Garden: Common-sense Guide to Vegetable Gardening for the Modern Homeowner.** 1979. Harpswell Press, Brunswick, ME. An introductory how-to for the beginning gardener that covers the basics like soil building, composting, fertilizer, seeds, etc.

Van Cleave, Janice, **Janice Van Cleave's Biology for Every Kid.** 1990. John Wiley and Sons, Inc. Experiments for the elementary student covering plants, animals, and humans.

Walking Night Bear and Stan Padilla, **Song of the Seven Herbs.** 1983. Book Publishing Co. Seven Native American stories about the origins of seven different plants. A great way to introduce students to some of the beliefs found in Native American cultures.

Zim, Herbert S., **What's Inside of Plants**. 1952. William Morrow & Co., NY, NY. Illustrations can be used by young children to understand the fascinating world of plants. Large-type and small-type pages appropriate for readers of varying levels.

Food Works

Food Works is an educational non-profit organizational based in Montpelier, Vermont. Through its Common Roots Program, Food Works staff offers courses, workshops, and guidebooks for developing community-based curriculum that focuses on the local natural and cultural heritage.

Food Works is committed to working with teachers to adapt their state and district learning standards to fit each community's unique ecological, cultural, and agricultural history, including the traditional knowledge, skills, and stories that have been passed down through the generations. Children naturally cultivate a strong sense of purpose in their lives when they can build their own sense of place by learning the ecological teachings of the natural world.

**Food Works
Common Roots Press
64 Main Street
Montpelier, VT 05602
(802) 223-1515
rootsnet@plainfield.bypass.com**

PROFESSIONAL DEVELOPMENT COURSES
Schools & Communities Rediscovering Their Common Roots

Agricultural Literacy: Master Gardening Course for Teachers

Research has shown that students demonstrate significant improvements in motivation and self-esteem both in and out of the classroom by growing, harvesting, and eating their own food. This innovative three-credit adapted master gardener course provides K–8 teachers with cross-curriculum horticultural content, hands-on classroom gardening activities, and the tools for creating a seasonal, integrated standards-based unit. Drawing on their state and district learning standards, participants design innovative activities for creating an indoor and outdoor garden based on the agricultural heritage of the local school community.

Ecological Literacy: Schoolyard Habitats and Nature Trails

The Ecological Literacy Course is based on a comprehensive system for studying and assessing continuity and change in the natural environment. By becoming active participants in the study, preservation, and restoration of local habitats, students have demonstrated renewed excitement in their own learning process through these comprehensive ecological literacy activities.

The course is an integrated curriculum development process focusing on the essential connections between the natural and cultural heritage of communities. Using sound ecological principles, the hands-on interdisciplinary learning units developed through this course align to national, state, and district academic standards across the subject areas for grades K–12.

Cultural Literacy: Hands-on Local History

Cultural literacy is an understanding of the literature, lore, common stories, age-old knowledge, religious beliefs, and folkways of our recent and distant past. Knowing the cultural heritage of a school's community means learning the local legends, crafts, traditional skills, agriculture, arts, music, dance, religious traditions, and beliefs of the surrounding town, city, and neighborhood.

This course takes teachers through a clear, step-by-step process for integrating local history into standards-based school curriculum drawing from local resources including libraries, museums, and historical societies, as well as the skills and experience of community members including elders, artisans, storytellers, parents, and others.

To Enroll

Contact us at the address at left. Courses and workshops are held at our Central Vermont location or they can be brought directly to your school or district on a first-come, first-serve basis. Call or write our Vermont office to become part of a growing network of schools and communities creating a living curriculum that stimulates the natural curiosity of children to explore the world around them.

COMMON ROOTS CURRICULUM GUIDEBOOKS

Making Outdoor Education WORK in Schools

Thousands of teachers and curriculum specialists from around the country have been using these path-breaking guidebooks to lead their elementary-aged students in seasonal, hands-on explorations in the natural environment.

Digging Deeper: Integrating Youth Gardens into Schools & Communities, A Comprehensive Guide

Called by Vermont Education Commissioner Dr. Marc Hull "an invaluable resource for all educators interested in making learning come to life for their students," *Digging Deeper* contains dozens of academic activities and project ideas for the curious student out in the garden and in nature. $19.95

To Order

To order books by phone, e-mail, or mail, contact Food Works at the address at left.

In The Three Sisters Garden

Sister Corn, Sister Squash, and Sister Bean introduce children to gardening in a year-long adventure that explores the ancient wisdom of the land. This unique journey through the seasons is rich with earth-friendly gardening methods, natural history lessons, and learning activities spanning the curriculum, including age-old legends and provocative new project ideas. $28.95

The Wonderful World of Wigglers

Integrated hands-on activities and projects help children understand the fundamental relationships between earthworms, soil, and local ecology. $14.95

Exploring the Secrets of the Meadow-Thicket

Throughout the seasons, children are guided on a journey of wonder filled with stories, activities, and learning adventures. The seasonal rhythms of a constantly changing landscape are discovered and celebrated. $18.95

Exploring the Forest with Grandforest Tree

Grandforest Tree, who is very old and very wise, unfolds the story of the forest and its many mysteries, providing children with dozens of exciting hands-on, hearts-on activities to learn from and enjoy. $18.95

The Indoor River Book

This first-of-its-kind guide is a simple step-by-step teachers' manual for building an indoor aquatic habitat modeled after the local watershed. For grades 4 and up, the book includes activities in the sciences, design technology, natural history, math, plus social studies and the arts. $14.95

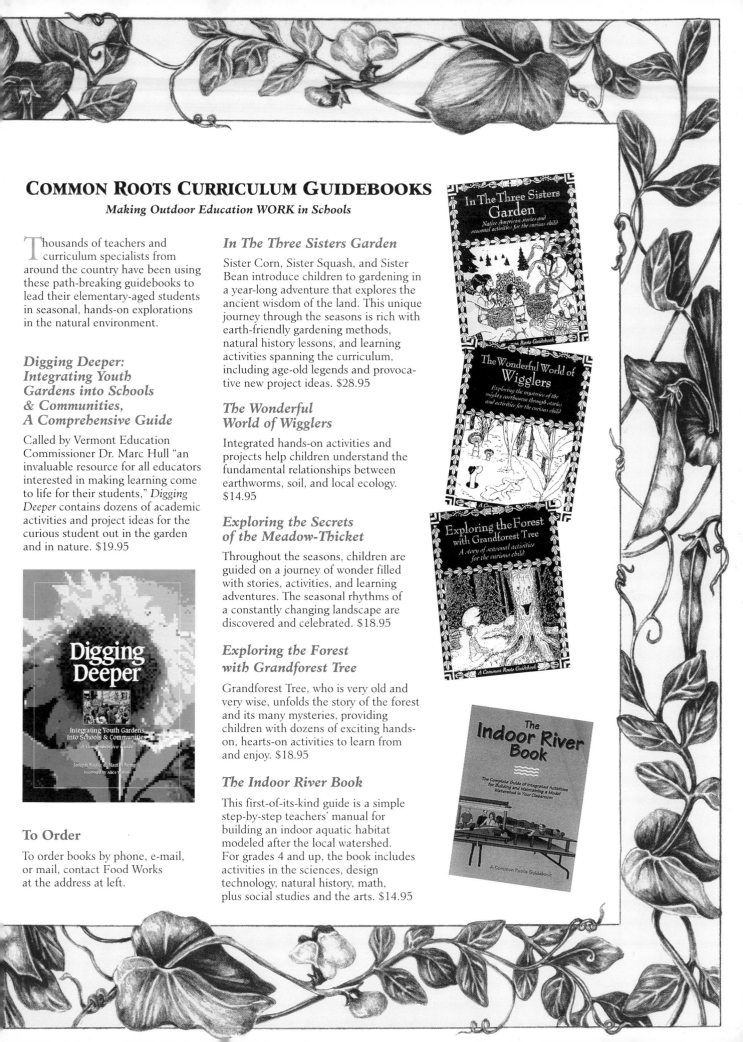

Help Young Minds Grow

with support from
the National Gardening Association

Youth Garden Grants Program

Each year, we award at least 300 schools and youth groups $700 worth of tools, seeds, equipment, and educational materials to help initiate or sustain gardening programs. Consideration is given for innovative programming, sustainability, community support, strong leadership, and need. The deadline for applications is November 15. (You can request an application, or download one from our Web site.)

Growing Ideas: A Journal of Garden-Based Learning

This 12-page newsletter is a rich source of project ideas, resources, and teaching strategies for using plants and gardens as living laboratories. Thematic how-to articles cover topics from butterfly gardens to school compost projects, drawing on experiences from classrooms across the country. Contact us to request a free sample issue.

Kids and Classrooms Web Site

Through our World Wide Web site, you can order materials from the Growing Ideas catalog, read articles from back issues of the *Growing Ideas* newsletter, and exchange information with e-mail pals from other gardening classrooms. The site also features information on grants and links to other plant- and garden-based sites. You'll find us at *http://www.garden.org/edu*

GrowLab Science Program

GrowLab is a National Science Foundation-funded program that includes indoor garden laboratories, curriculum materials that align with the National Science Education Standards, and a national network of training consultants. Its inquiry-based teaching approach helps students learn to think and act like scientists, using their own questions and observations as a springboard for learning.

Growing Ideas Catalog: Teaching Tools to Help Young Minds Grow

Our exemplary educational materials help educators cultivate a love of learning. Includes: worm bins and curricula, hydroponic units, GrowLab indoor gardens and supplies, resources for multicultural, handicapped, and early childhood gardening programs, FastPlant and Bottle Biology books, school greenhouse kits, and *NGA's Guide to Kids' Gardening*.

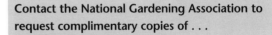

Contact the National Gardening Association to request complimentary copies of . . .

• Youth Garden Grant application
• *Growing Ideas* newsletter
• GrowLab Program information
• *Growing Ideas* catalog

National Gardening Association
180 Flynn Avenue
Burlington, VT 05401
1-800-538-7476; e-mail: eddept@garden.org
Web site: *www.garden.org*

❧ *Feed Us Back* ❦

While this book has a conclusion, this is neither the end nor the beginning of our story; it is merely one element of an ongoing natural cycle that has sustained humans for thousands of years. Digging deeper begins with each one of us and seeds itself along the way in the hearts and minds of everyone we touch. The next installment of the story requires you who are reading this now to share your trials and triumphs growing with children. Based on your feedback describing the educational, cultural, and environmental outcomes of this growing ecological gardening movement, we plan to highlight, in the next edition of this book, regional case studies that demonstrate the impact of gardens on children's ways of learning and living.

We want to hear from you to create an educational clearinghouse of garden activities, projects, and standards-based units that meet the needs of learners of all ages. Your feedback describing your experiences of gardening with children will strengthen the burgeoning Garden in Every School movement as a living example of ecological education in action. Our aim is to facilitate the redesign of school grounds and open public spaces into educational landscapes that will serve as local centers for food and ecological research, demonstration, and community learning.

So please, take a few moments to answer the following questions and send us your responses, stories, ideas, questions, and comments.

ECOLOGICAL GARDENING IN ACTION

1. How have you used this book to develop a children's gardening program? Please explain.
2. Describe any food and garden units that you have developed that are linked to your state or district learning standards. Specify grade levels, geographical region, theme of garden, how the garden is used to teach existing curriculum, seasons of use, obstacles or challenges addressed, examples of community service and entrepreneurial activities, and garden designs.
3. As an educator and youth gardening coordinator, what other questions, information, activities, ideas, and designs would you like included in a follow-up ecological education garden guide to help you in your work?
4. Please include photos: before/during/after
5. Send material to Food Works, 64 Main Street, Montpelier, Vermont 05602